Russia Moves into the Global Economy

> Letiche's book is a fine analysis, of interest to all observers of new world economic trends.
>
> Lawrence R. Klein, Nobel Laureate in Economics

> Professor Letiche's book is certainly the most comprehensive and up-to-date review of the important economic and political developments currently taking place in Russia. It also has the merit of being well documented, carefully balanced, and quite provocative in its analysis and conclusions. His analysis of the developments in the energy sector is of particular interest in this context.
>
> Jacques R. Artus, Former Deputy of the European Department, I.M.F.

Russia is breaking out from historic cataclysms into the global economy. This book is necessary reading for anyone with an interest in what is really happening in Russia today.

Three phases are identified and explored in Russia's successful economic transition. The first is associated predominantly with an effective depreciation in the value of the ruble. The second is driven primarily by the sharp rise in world energy prices. The third phase represents a continuum of phase one and two, with successes and setbacks of President Putin's administration. Thus, the concluding part of this study considers longer-term reforms in both economic and non-economic areas.

The book will benefit undergraduate as well as graduate students of subjects such as international economics, Russian and eastern European politics and economics.

John M. Letiche is Professor Emeritus of Economics at the University of California, Berkeley.

Routledge studies in the modern world economy

1 **Interest Rates and Budget Deficits**
A study of the advanced economies
Kanhaya L. Gupta and Bakhtiar Moazzami

2 **World Trade after the Uruguay Round**
Prospects and policy options for the twenty-first century
Edited by Harald Sander and András Inotai

3 **The Flow Analysis of Labour Markets**
Edited by Ronald Schettkat

4 **Inflation and Unemployment**
Contributions to a new macroeconomic approach
Edited by Alvaro Cencini and Mauro Baranzini

5 **Macroeconomic Dimensions of Public Finance**
Essays in honour of Vito Tanzi
Edited by Mario I. Blejer and Teresa M. Ter-Minassian

6 **Fiscal Policy and Economic Reforms**
Essays in honour of Vito Tanzi
Edited by Mario I. Blejer and Teresa M. Ter-Minassian

7 **Competition Policy in the Global Economy**
Modalities for co-operation
Edited by Leonard Waverman, William S. Comanor and Akira Goto

8 **Working in the Macro Economy**
A study of the US labor market
Martin F.J. Prachowny

9 **How Does Privatization Work?**
Edited by Anthony Bennett

10 **The Economics and Politics of International Trade**
Freedom and trade: volume II
Edited by Gary Cook

11 **The Legal and Moral Aspects of International Trade**
Freedom and trade: volume III
Edited by Asif Qureshi, Hillel Steiner and Geraint Parry

12 **Capital Markets and Corporate Governance in Japan, Germany and the United States**
Organizational response to market inefficiencies
Helmut M. Dietl

13 **Competition and Trade Policies**
Coherence or conflict
Edited by Einar Hope

14 **Rice**
The primary commodity
A.J.H. Latham

15 **Trade, Theory and Econometrics**
Essays in honour of John S. Chipman
Edited by James C. Moore, Raymond Riezman and James R. Melvin

16 **Who Benefits from Privatisation?**
Edited by Moazzem Hossain and Justin Malbon

17 **Towards a Fair Global Labour Market**
Avoiding the new slave trade
Ozay Mehmet, Errol Mendes and Robert Sinding

18 **Models of Futures Markets**
Edited by Barry Goss

19 **Venture Capital Investment**
An agency analysis of UK practice
Gavin C. Reid

20 **Macroeconomic Forecasting**
A sociological appraisal
Robert Evans

21 **Multimedia and Regional Economic Restructuring**
Edited by Hans-Joachim Braczyk, Gerhard Fuchs and Hans-Georg Wolf

22 **The New Industrial Geography**
Regions, regulation and institutions
Edited by Trevor J. Barnes and Meric S. Gertler

23 **The Employment Impact of Innovation**
Evidence and policy
Edited by Marco Vivarelli and Mario Pianta

24 **International Health Care Reform**
A legal, economic and political analysis
Colleen Flood

25 **Competition Policy Analysis**
Edited by Einar Hope

26 **Culture and Enterprise**
The development, representation and morality of business
Don Lavoie and Emily Chamlee-Wright

27 **Global Financial Crises and Reforms**
Cases and caveats
B.N. Ghosh

28 **Geography of Production and Economic Integration**
Miroslav N. Jovanović

29 **Technology, Trade and Growth in OECD Countries**
Does specialisation matter?
Valentina Meliciani

30 **Post-Industrial Labour Markets**
Profiles of North America and Scandinavia
Edited by Thomas P. Boje and Bengt Furaker

31 **Capital Flows without Crisis**
Reconciling capital mobility and economic stability
Edited by Dipak Dasgupta, Marc Uzan and Dominic Wilson

32 **International Trade and National Welfare**
Murray C. Kemp

33 **Global Trading Systems at Crossroads**
A post-Seattle perspective
Dilip K. Das

34 **The Economics and Management of Technological Diversification**
Edited by John Cantwell, Alfonso Gambardella and Ove Granstrand

35 **Before and Beyond EMU**
Historical lessons and future prospects
Edited by Patrick Crowley

36 **Fiscal Decentralization**
Ehtisham Ahmad and Vito Tanzi

37 **Regionalisation of Globalised Innovation**
Locations for advanced industrial development and disparities in participation
Edited by Ulrich Hilpert

38 **Gold and the Modern World Economy**
Edited by MoonJoong Tcha

39 **Global Economic Institutions**
Willem Molle

40 **Global Governance and Financial Crises**
Edited by Meghnad Desai and Yahia Said

41 **Linking Local and Global Economies**
The ties that bind
Edited by Carlo Pietrobelli and Arni Sverrisson

42 Tax Systems and Tax Reforms in Europe
Edited by Luigi Bernardi and Paola Profeta

43 Trade Liberalization and APEC
Edited by Jiro Okamoto

44 Fiscal Deficits in the Pacific Region
Edited by Akira Kohsaka

45 Financial Globalization and the Emerging Market Economies
Dilip K. Das

46 International Labor Mobility
Unemployment and increasing returns to scale
Bharati Basu

47 Good Governance in the Era of Global Neoliberalism
Conflict and depolitization in Latin America, Eastern Europe, Asia and Africa
Edited by Jolle Demmers, Alex E. Fernández Jilberto and Barbara Hogenboom

48 The International Trade System
Alice Landau

49 International Perspectives on Temporary Work and Workers
Edited by John Burgess and Julia Connell

50 Working Time and Workers' Preferences in Industrialized Countries
Finding the balance
Edited by Jon C. Messenger

51 Tax Systems and Tax Reforms in New EU Members
Edited by Luigi Bernardi, Mark Chandler and Luca Gandullia

52 Globalization and the Nation State
The impact of the IMF and the World Bank
Edited by Gustav Ranis, James Vreeland and Stephen Kosak

53 Macroeconomic Policies and Poverty Reduction
Edited by Ashoka Mody and Catherine Pattillo

54 Regional Monetary Policy
Carlos J. Rodríguez-Fuentez

55 Trade and Migration in the Modern World
Carl Mosk

56 Globalisation and the Labour Market
Trade, technology and less-skilled workers in Europe and the United States
Edited by Robert Anderton, Paul Brenton and John Whalley

57 **Financial Crises**
Socio-economic causes and institutional context
Brenda Spotton Visano

58 **Globalization and Self-Determination**
Is the nation-state under siege?
Edited by David R. Cameron, Gustav Ranis and Annalisa Zinn

59 **Developing Countries and the Doha Development Round of the WTO**
Edited by Pitou van Dijck and Gerrit Faber

60 **Immigrant Enterprise in Europe and the USA**
Prodromos Panayiotopoulos

61 **Solving the Riddle of Globalization and Development**
Edited by Manuel Agosín, David Bloom, George Chapelier and Jagdish Saigal

62 **Foreign Direct Investment and the World Economy**
Ashoka Mody

63 **The World Economy**
A global analysis
Horst Siebert

64 **Production Organizations in Japanese Economic Development**
Edited by Tetsuji Okazaki

65 **The Economics of Language**
International analyses
Edited by Barry R. Chiswick and Paul W. Miller

66 **Street Entrepreneurs**
People, place and politics in local and global perspective
Edited by John Cross and Alfonso Morales

67 **Global Challenges and Local Responses**
The East Asian experience
Edited by Jang-Sup Shin

68 **Globalization and Regional Integration**
The origins, development and impact of the single European aviation market
Alan P. Dobson

69 **Russia Moves into the Global Economy**
John M. Letiche

Russia Moves into the Global Economy

John M. Letiche

LONDON AND NEW YORK

First published 2007
by Routledge
2 Park Square, Milton Park, Abingdon, Oxon OX14 4RN

Simultaneously published in the USA and Canada
by Routledge
605 Third Avenue, New York, NY 10017

Routledge is an imprint of the Taylor & Francis Group, an informa business

© 2007 John M. Letiche

Typeset in Times by Wearset Ltd, Boldon, Tyne and Wear

All rights reserved. No part of this book may be reprinted or
reproduced or utilized in any form or by any electronic,
mechanical or other means, now known or hereafter invented,
including photocopying and recording, or in any information
storage or retrieval system, without permission in writing from the
publishers.

Notice:
Product or corporate names may be trademarks or registered trademarks, and are
used only for identification and explanation without intent to infringe.

British Library Cataloguing in Publication Data
A catalogue record for this book is available from the British Library

Library of Congress Cataloging in Publication Data
A catalog record for this book has been requested

ISBN13: 978-0-415-77054-5 (hbk)
ISBN13: 978-0-415-49417-5 (pbk)
ISBN13: 978-0-203-94658-9 (ebk)

Contents

Illustrations

Figures

Tables

Preface

The aim of this study is to explain the present state of Russia's political economy in the light of the past, for the future. Three phases have been identified in Russia's successful economic transition since the crisis of August 1998. Phase one was associated predominantly with an effective depreciation in the value of the ruble, which is a necessary condition for macroeconomic stabilization. It brought Russia's cost-price structure – in the non-energy fields – in line with international competitive conditions. This phase had practically nothing to do with the price of oil. Phase two was driven primarily by the sharp rise in world energy prices. The third phase represented a continuum of phases one and two, with successes and setbacks of President Putin's administration. This phase incorporated, as much as intellectual decencies permit, an objective analysis of the Yukos crisis. The evidence indicates that the crisis had a seriously damaging effect on the performance of the Russian economy.

Russia, it is shown, suffers from a trilemma: a quasi-market economy, a destructive bureaucracy and systemic corruption. If President Putin's goal of doubling Russia's GDP by 2012 is to be achieved, key economic reforms are indispensable. This study therefore includes a section on necessary basic principles of a successful Russian market economy.

Tensions and divisions have recently been intensified between Western governments and the Kremlin. Thus, the concluding part of this study considers longer-term reforms in both the economic and non-economic areas. I have placed special emphasis on Russia's accession to the WTO as a means of expediting its integration into the European-Atlantic Community.

It is a pleasure to thank Zhores I. Alferov, Director of Research, Ioffe Physico-Technical Institute, St. Petersburg, for inviting me to deliver a keynote address on the topics at hand at the Institute's eightieth anniversary, thereby generating the basis for this study. On several occasions, Alferov also arranged interviews for me with Russian economists, government officials and members of the Duma. I am particularly grateful to the following for discussions and material that otherwise would have been unavailable to me: L.I. Abalkin, Aleksei Kuprianov, D.S. Lvov, V.L. Makarov and A.D. Nekipelov. Aleksei Arbatov served as a visiting lecturer at the University of California at Berkeley and presented an insider's view of Russian conditions and parliamentary procedures. Acknowledgement is due to Lawrence R. Klein for constant inspiration and exchange of views. Klein, Jacques Artus, Ellison Berg, George F. Break, George W. Breslauer and Donald S. Lamm read the manuscript and offered insightful comments. To my friends and colleagues I am indebted for intellectual stimulus and professional counsel, particularly to Kazuko K. Artus, Pranab Bardhan, Helen Break, Barry Eichengreen, Gregory Grossman, Maurice Obstfeld, Gerard Roland, Lloyd Ulman and Oliver Williamson. Robert Keyfitz at the World Bank kindly supplied me with invaluable information. Stanley Marcus provided professional editorial service. Basil Dmytryshyn gave me expert advice on translating Russian sources. Jim Church and John Kupersmith furnished exemplary library assistance, and Arnold Yip provided draftsmanship. To my wife Emily K. Letiche, I am deeply thankful for her literary criticism and to my friends Louise Sullivan and Aaron Crump for their personal interest in preparing the typescript.

This study has been an ongoing endeavor for seven years, with three extensive visits to Russia, and I greatly hope that the reader will have occasion to share my satisfaction at its completion.

1 Russia's economic restructuring since the 1998 crisis

Introduction

A primary objective of this study is to analyze the key factors responsible for Russia's successful economic transition since the crisis of August 1998, factors that have frequently been misinterpreted. The study is in two parts. Part one examines Russia's restructuring in the period from late 1998 to 2005, discusses the continuing effects of the economic legacies of the 1990s, and records the influence of President Vladimir V. Putin on the transition.[1] Part two presents the basic principles applicable to the creation of a successful Russian market economy for the long term and recommends policies for integrating the Russian economy with the European-Atlantic community. The main economic indicators and the new statistical data relevant to Russia's economic condition have been placed in an appendix.

Three sets of forces have marked the process of Russia's economic transition since the crisis of August 1998. First, from about the third quarter of 1998 until the third quarter of 1999, the economic restructuring was primarily associated with a sharp real depreciation of the ruble. Second, thereafter, and especially until the third quarter of 2000, it was principally related to the rise in world energy prices. Third, the joint operation of these two forces in an enabling environment – though with some recent setbacks – has generated cumulative effects conducive to Russia's long-term economic growth.

As can be seen in Figure 1.1, which indicates the real GDP growth rate of the world, United States, China, Poland and Russia from 1991 to 2005, Russia's economic performance from the end of 1998 to 2000 was truly outstanding. Its real GDP growth rate rose from –5.3 percent in 1998 to 6.3 percent in 1999 and 10.0 percent in 2000 – stabilizing at an average rate of about 6.1 percent in 2001 through 2005.

Russia's economic performance during most of the 1990s was

catastrophic: as seen in Table 1.1, the level of its real GDP in 1998 was 40.3 percent below that of 1991. During the period 1990–1999, Russia's real GDP growth rate was negative in every year but one – 1997 – when it grew at a lackluster rate of 1.4 percent. The percent of total population in poverty rose from a Soviet recorded 2.0 percent in 1987–1988 to 50 percent in 1993–1995.[2]

In the period 1991–1997, there was no correlation between Russia's real GDP growth rate and that of the world. But from 1997 to 2000 such correlation began to occur (Figure 1.1). The causes and consequences of Russia's dismal economic performance during most of the 1990s have been extensively discussed in the literature.[3] The purpose of this analysis is to examine the main reasons for the change from economic depression to economic advance.

Overvalued currencies have been a recurring curse in economic history. In late 1991, at the time of dissolution of the Soviet Union, the ruble was an immensely overvalued, pegged exchange rate. As is shown in Appendix III, Table III.3, it was then pegged at one ruble=$5.19. Although the ruble was periodically devalued during the period 1991–1995, Russia's rate of inflation greatly exceeded the rate of devaluation.[4] Further, on a base of 1995–1997=100, the real effective exchange rate rose from an index of 84.9 in 1995 to an index of 106.7 in 1997.[5]

Despite the overvalued ruble, Russia's merchandise trade balance was positive throughout this period. The nation enjoyed huge comparative advantages in fuel, metals and wood/paper products; exports of these and other natural-resource products rose from 65 percent of total exports in

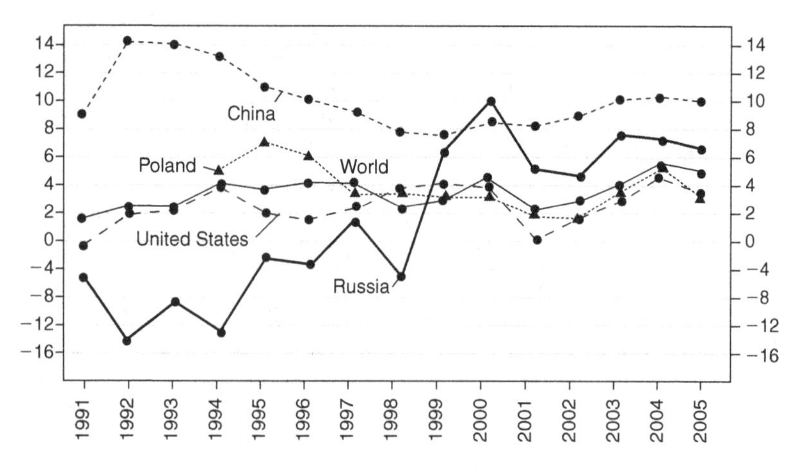

Figure 1.1 Real GDP growth rate: World, United States, China, Poland and Russia, 1991–2005.

Table 1.1a Russian federation: real GDP in United States (1990) – international dollars and real GDP growth rate 1989–2005

1989	1,208.4	—
1990	1,172.1	–3.0
1991	1,113.5	–5.0
1992	1,057.8	–14.5
1993	904.4	–8.7
1994	825.7	–12.7
1995	720.8	–4.0
1996	692.0	–3.6
1997	701.7	1.4
1998	664.5	–5.3
1999	706.4	6.3
2000	777.0	10.0
2001	816.6	5.1
2002	855.0	4.7
2003	917.4	7.3
2004	983.5	7.2
2005	1,046.4	6.4

Sources: This series has been derived on the basis of data for the Russian Federation in Angus Maddison, *The World Economy, a Millennial Perspective, 0–1998 A.D.* (Paris OECD, 2000), Table 2–23, p. 156, for 1998 GDP in billion 1990 international U.S. dollars. The data for 1989–1997 were calculated on the base of this 1998 figure and the real GDP growth rate, annual percent change, as presented in OECD, *Macroeconomic Indicators* (Paris, 2001). The data for 1999–2005 were calculated on the base of the 1998 figure and the GDP growth rate, annual percent change, as presented in IMF, *World Economic Outlook* (Washington, DC, April 2004), Table 6, p. 195; OECD (*Economic Outlook*) Paris, December 2004), vol. 2004/2, no. 76, Table 1, p. 167, Table III, 3, p. 118, and OECD (*Economic Outlook*, December 2005), p. 122.

Table 1.1b Russian federation: GDP in terms of PPP – current international dollars (billion)

1989	*1990*	*1991*	*1992*	*1993*	*1994*	*1995*	*1996*	*1997*
1,302.5	1,274.4	1,241.8	1,151.2	1,045.3	921.5	914.1	893.1	902.6

1998	*1999*	*2000*	*2001*	*2002*	*2003*	*2004*	*2005*
869.3	766.8	1,056.8	1,107.7	1,141.9	1,306.6	1,424.4	1,539.0

Sources: World Bank, *World Development Indicators*, 2004; CIA, *World Factbook* (Washington DC, 2006), estimate for 2005.

1994 to 73.3 percent in 1997.[6] However, exports of most non-natural-resource products – machinery, equipment, (including cars) and instruments – remained relatively stagnant at 9.8 percent of total exports in 1994 and 10.2 percent in 1998.[7] Moreover, an analysis by Russian economists on "Export Windfall Calculations" concluded that while the windfall from total exports in percent of GDP was positive in 1995, amounting to 3.2 percent of GDP, it had turned negative in 1996, 1997 and 1998, amounting to –1.1, –1.6 and –43.3 percent, respectively, of GDP.[8] Clearly, the real effective overvaluation of the ruble was generated jointly by the pegged exchange rate regime in an environment of relative inflation and by a natural-resource export structure in a form traditionally known as the "Dutch disease" or the "oil curse."

The overvalued ruble had, *inter alia*, a devastating effect on Russia's agricultural production and composition of imports. As is shown in Appendix III and Appendix IV, on a base of 1990 = 100, at the time of the 1998 crisis agricultural production had declined by more than 50 percent. Considering Russia's potentially rich agricultural resources, the urgent need to modernize its agriculture is reflected in the high proportion of its food and agricultural imports: they constituted 22.2 percent of total imports in 1993 and rose to 28.3 percent by 1995.[9] As another sign of Russia's depression in the 1990s, imports of machinery and equipment as a percentage of total imports had declined from 37.7 percent in 1992 to 31.7 percent in 1996.[10]

From the time of the crisis until the end of 1999, on the basis of unit labor costs, the ruble had depreciated in terms of the dollar by about 70 percent, and on the basis of the consumer price index by 45 percent (Figure 1.2).[11] The rise in domestic prices relative to money wages, combined with the increase in productivity and the substantial excess capacity in manufacturing, raised profits in practically all industries. Average profits in industry increased by over 15 percent in 1999. Industrial output rose in 84 out of 89 regions and included most sectors.[12]

As can be seen in Figure 1.3, Russia's post-crisis economic transition has occurred in three phases. In phase one, which began in late 1998 and lasted until mid-1999, the recovery in output was driven by import substitution, not by the energy sector. In the second half of 1998, total merchandise imports (in billion U.S. dollars) fell by at least 50 percent. The volume of non-energy exports also gradually increased; though with the depreciated ruble, the dollar value of total exports in 1999 was about the same as in 1998. It was primarily the real depreciation of the ruble that brought Russia's cost-price structure – in the non-energy fields – into line with international competitive conditions. As a result, in 1999 the foreign trade balance surged.

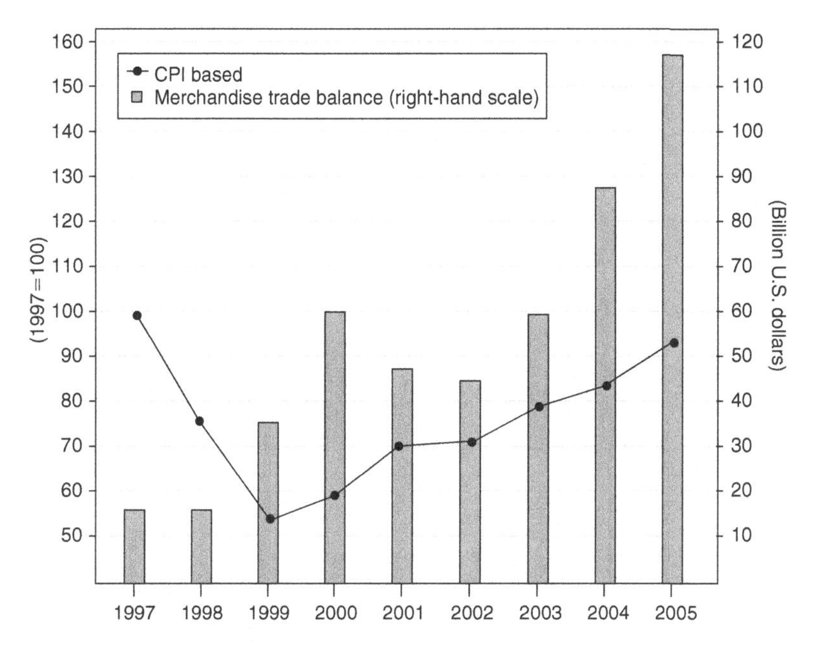

Figure 1.2 Russian federation: real exchange rate index, ruble/dollar and merchandise trade balance, 1997–2005.

The rise in profits and in retained earnings generated an expansion of investment in both industry and agriculture. Whereas gross investment had declined by 28.7 percent in 1998, it increased by 8.5 percent in 1999.[13] Moreover, some of the improvement in net profits was accounted for by a reduction in gross losses that had occurred primarily in the non-energy sectors.[14]

On a year-on-year basis, Russia's real GDP grew by $41.9 billion in 1999, while its energy exports increased only by $3.1 billion. Manifestly, energy exports had contributed much less to the first phase of Russia's post-crisis economic transition than did the improvement in the external balance and the related increase in domestic investment and output that were principally associated with the real effective depreciation of the ruble.

The second phase of the economic transition, which began after the middle of 1999 and lasted until the third quarter of 2000, was driven primarily by the sharp rise in world energy prices. The average dollar price of Russia's energy exports had declined by 37 percent from January 1997 to February 1999, but by September 2000 it had risen to 10 percent above the January 1997 level.[15] The price of Russia's crude oil was $15.79 a barrel

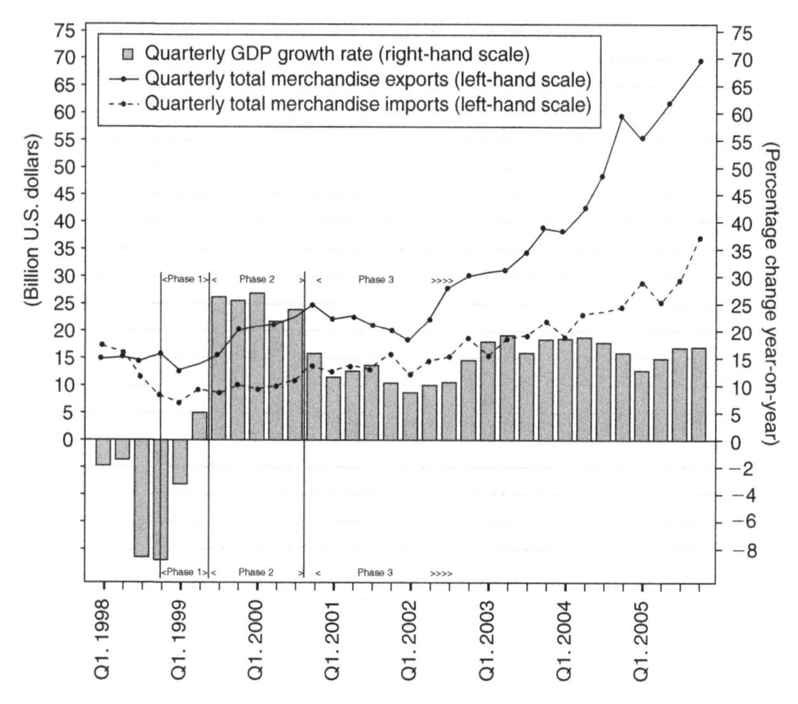

Figure 1.3 Russian federation: real quarterly GDP growth rate and quarterly change in total merchandise exports and imports, 1998–2005.

in 1998; the price in 1999 averaged $10.09 a barrel, but it rose to $24.70 a barrel in 2000 (Figure 1.4). The value of Russia's energy exports (oil, oil products and gas) rose rapidly thereafter, accounting in 2005 for about 63 percent of the value of Russia's total merchandise exports.[16] Gradually, more diversified channels of production have been developing, linking fluctuations in world energy prices to fluctuations in Russia's economic activity. In the very short term, however, the rise in world energy prices after mid-1999 had little effect on Russia's energy production: Output was constrained by bottlenecks in extraction and transportation, as well as by government policy that regulated the volume of sales at below world prices in the domestic markets.[17] Consequently, in 1999, on a year-on-year basis, Russia's oil production rose only 0.3 percent.[18] But the continued rise in world oil and gas prices from about the second half of 1999 to most of 2000 had a direct effect on increasing Russia's energy production, especially in 2001. Rising profits and retained earnings generated an expansion of domestic and foreign investment in exploration for, and output of, both oil and gas.

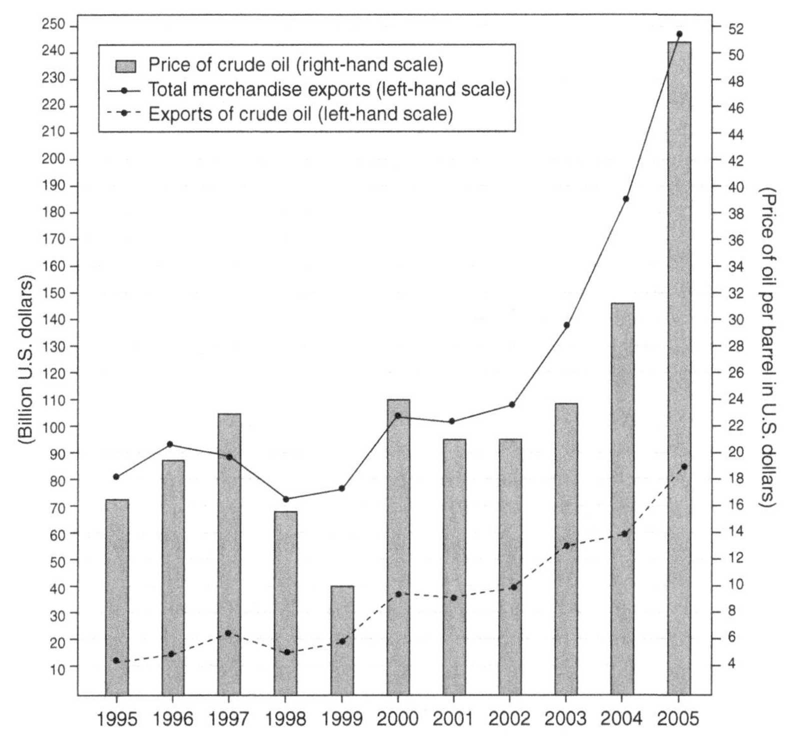

Figure 1.4 Russian federation: price of oil, exports of crude oil and total merchandise exports, 1995–2005.

Furthermore, most energy companies set about improving their infrastructure, thereby stimulating demand for domestically produced oil pipe and numerous complementary inputs. The beneficiaries, those in the aluminum industry, have utilized their retained earnings to diversify production downstream. In a number of cases, they have extended their focus from natural resource production to processing. Cumulative multiplier effects have followed in many sectors. Russia's real GDP grew by 10 percent in 2000, an increase of $70.6 billion from 1999 (Table 1.1). Its energy exports grew by 10.3 percent in 2000, an increase of $21.8 billion from 1999.[19]

The third phase of the post-crisis transition, which began in the third quarter of 2000 and has been ongoing for more than five years, represents a continuation of the second phase, benefiting now from the considerable politico-economic stabilization promoted by President Putin; however, as will be shown, the second half of 2004 brought about some serious setbacks.

When Putin was named prime minister in 1999, as already noted, economic conditions in Russia were beginning to improve, although the nation was still in a perilous state. His own judgment on the conditions of the time was revealed in his comment, "If I can help save Russia from *collapse*, then I'll have something to be proud of."[20]

Widespread predictions to the contrary notwithstanding, the Central Bank of Russia (CBR) had made strong efforts – with considerable success – to rein in the inflationary pressures associated with the economic crisis of 1998. But the CBR was substantially beholden to myriad vested interests in the Duma that were promoting enlarged government expenditures. A marked improvement in financial conditions could not be achieved without cutting federal discretionary expenditures and improving compliance with the tax laws. Putin initiated comprehensive investigations to serve as a basis for such actions.

The evidence indicates that, even though banking reforms have seriously lagged behind schedule, from the time Putin became prime minister, the consumer price index (CPI) has been brought under control more effectively. On a seasonally adjusted basis, the average monthly CPI increase has been reduced to about 1 percent per month.[21] The fiscal system has been fundamentally and successfully transformed. In particular, the reduction of the income tax to a flat 13 percent and the corporate tax from 34 to 24 percent has had a spectacular effect on increasing tax compliance. Suffice it to note here that, from 1999 to 2001 Q3, government expenditure as a percentage of GDP was reduced by 2.6 points; government revenue as a percentage of GDP increased by 3.3 points; and the primary overall budget balance was reversed from a deficit of –4.3 percent of GDP to a surplus of 1.6 percent of GDP.[22] In 2002, the federal government balance was in surplus at 2.3 percent of GDP, and in 2003 it was at a surplus of 1.7 percent of GDP.[23]

The resulting increase in liquidity at all levels of the economy – government, firms, households – rendered it possible to slash enterprises' total arrears and tax arrears, as well as to reduce bilateral barter sales (Figures 1.5–1.7). According to official estimates, by 2002 industrial output had grown one-third since 1998, while industrial employment had hardly increased, indicating a substantial rise in labor productivity – albeit from extremely low levels (Appendix II).[24] Not surprisingly, the years 2000–2002 recorded a marked improvement in the popularity of the president (Figure 1.10). These indicators are a reflection of the turnaround that has occurred since 1999 in the annual percentage change in the real income per capita, in the real wage, in the real minimum wage and in real pensions (Appendix VII).

The oil sector and oil exports continued to expand in the third phase of

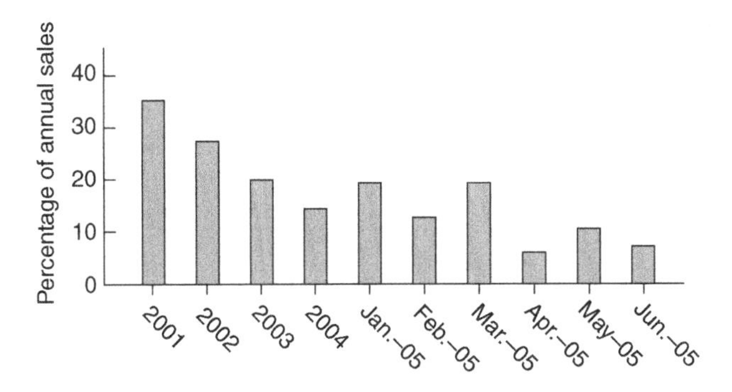

Figure 1.5 Stock of overdue payables, 2001–2005.

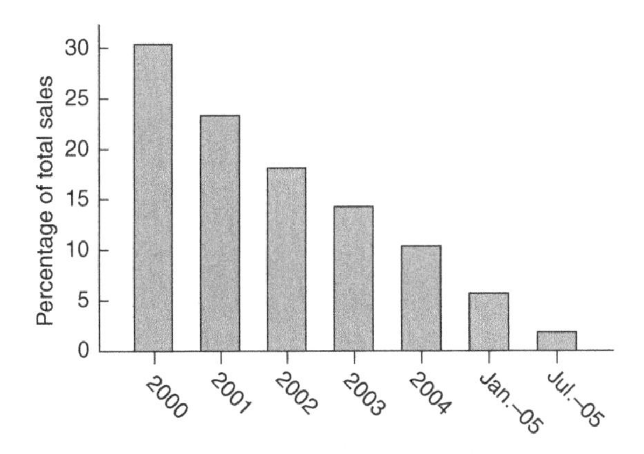

Figure 1.6 Non-cash settlements, 2000–2005.

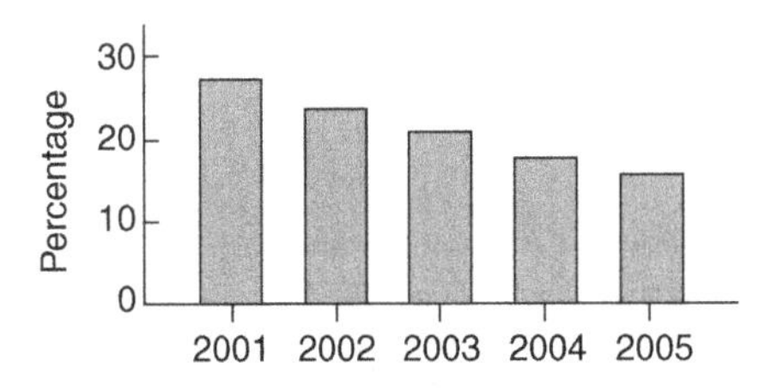

Figure 1.7 Share of people living below subsistent income, 2001–2005.

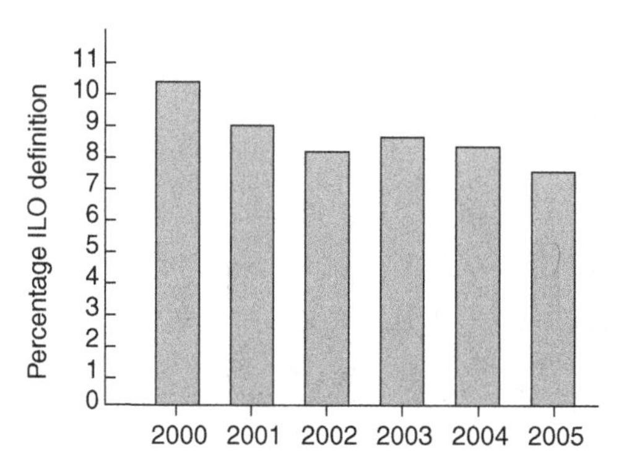

Figure 1.8 Unemployment, 2000–2005.

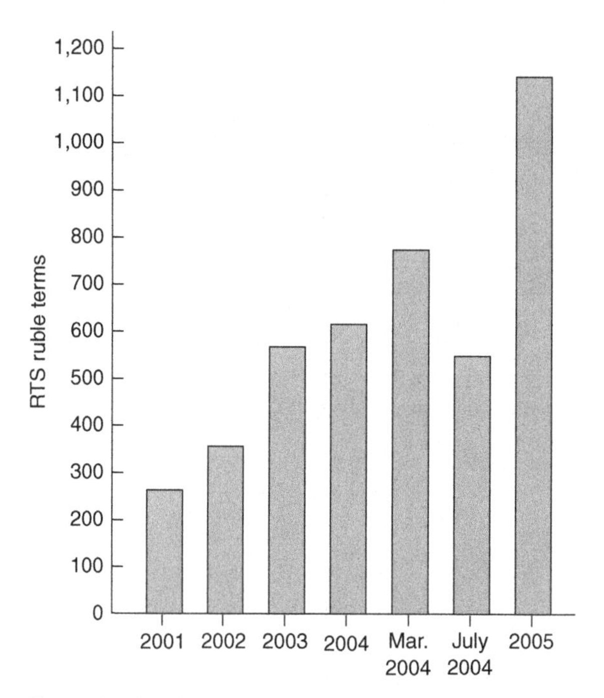

Figure 1.9 Stock market index, 2001–2005.

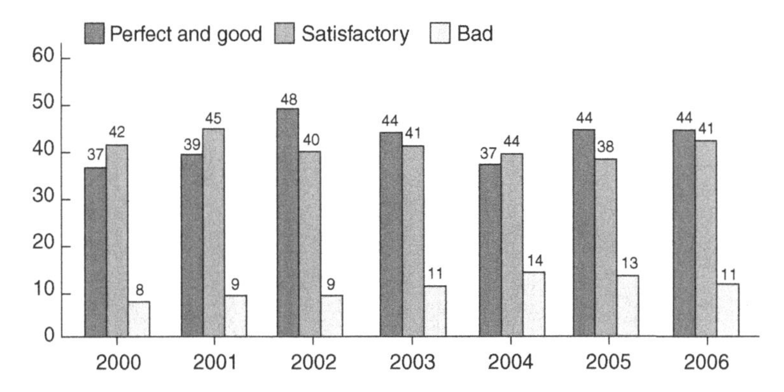

Figure 1.10 Popularity/evaluation rating of the president, 2000–2006 (as of May 2–5, 2006.

the transition, but the Russian economy is extremely sensitive to world oil prices. As shown in Figure 1.4, from 2000 to 2001, the average dollar price of Russian oil fell moderately and stabilized in 2002. Not only did the dollar value of Russia's oil exports fall from 2000 to 2001, but also did the dollar value of its total merchandise exports. From 2001 to 2002, the dollar value of both the country's oil exports and its total merchandise exports increased. However, from 2000 to 2002, the dollar value of Russia's imports steadily increased, resulting in a decline in the surplus of the trade balance (Figure 1.2 and Appendix VI). Clearly, the increase in the dollar value of imports has been associated with the joint rise in Russia's GDP and in the real effective exchange rate of the ruble in terms of the dollar.[25]

A salient feature of the third phase of the post-crisis transition has been the more rapid rate of growth in 2001 and 2002 in Russia's total domestic expenditures than in the rate of growth of its GDP (Figure 1.11). In 1999 and 2000, whereas GDP grew at the rate of 6.3 and 10 percent, respectively, domestic expenditures grew at the lower rate of 0.6 and 5.0 percent, respectively. In 2001 and 2002, however, GDP grew at the rate of 5.1 and 4.7 percent, respectively, while domestic expenditures grew at the higher rate of 7.3 and 5.6 percent, respectively. Thus in 2001 and 2002, rising domestic expenditures contributed at a more rapid pace than the external balance to Russia's real GDP growth rate.[26] Although the extraordinary rise in the world price of oil and gas since 2003 reversed this tendency, if energy prices decline to more moderate levels, the preceding new feature may be expected to return.

The combined effects of the real depreciation of the ruble, the high energy prices and the economic reforms have therefore led to a significant

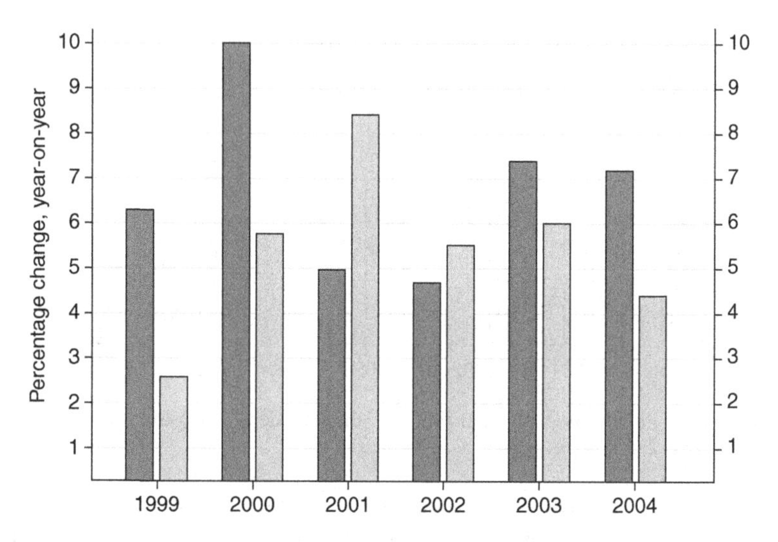

Figure 1.11 Russian federation: real GDP growth rate and real growth rate of total domestic expenditures, 1999–2004.

improvement in macroeconomic stability and in economic growth. These factors, jointly operating in the third phase of the post-crisis transition, have also encouraged domestic and foreign entrepreneurs to engage in partnerships of large-scale direct investment which, if well selected, well designed and well managed, are likely to have a singularly important impact on Russia's long-term economic development.

One comprehensive survey by the European Bank for Reconstruction and Development (EBRD), with the collaboration of the World Bank, concluded that in 2002 the Russian business environment had improved, enterprise performance had advanced and property rights as well as competitive markets had strengthened.[27] Some reduction was also recorded in crime and corruption. Another survey by the Center for Economic and Financial Research in Moscow found that new laws limiting government interference in small business had the effect of reducing paper work for many executives. But there was little improvement in business regulation or in the capacity of the government to *enforce* existing laws.[28] Generally, foreign investors reacted positively to the changes in Russia's economic climate.[29] Financial experts referred to the anticipated change in market profitability as a sign of confidence not only in the new Russian economic environment but also in the new management of many key Russian enterprises.[30]

This environment, as will be shown, was shattered in the fall of 2003 by zealous and disruptive prosecutorial activity. Financial markets were beset by uncertainty. Moscow's stock trading index (RTS) plummeted. The rate of growth in capital investment declined. Despite high world prices for oil and gas, Russia's GDP growth rate fell from 7.7 percent in the third quarter of 2003 to 6.7 percent in the third quarter of 2004 (Figure 1.3). Projections for Russia's GDP growth rate in the medium term by the IMF, OECD, the Russian government and private experts were significantly reduced. As Pekka Sutela, head of research, Institute for Economics in Transition (BOFIT), observed: the Bank of Finland's and other forecasters' basic scenario for the Russian economy is that it will grow at a rate of 4–5 percent in the medium term.[31] On January 31, 2006, at his annual news conference for more than 1,000 international journalists, President Putin expressed satisfaction that Russia had achieved a GDP growth rate of 6.4 percent in 2005 – the government had projected a growth rate of only 5.9 percent. Significantly, however, he proceeded to launch a new and comprehensive agenda for Russia's economic development in the medium and longer terms, the basic provisions of which are as follows.[32]

1 Russia will put into effect a program of innovative restructuring. Certain national projects will be given priority: education, health care, affordable housing and agriculture head the list. They are designed to reduce poverty and enhance development. Their financing and implementation are to be conducted jointly by the federal and regional authorities.
2 The presidential administration and the Duma will adopt measures to accelerate the diversification of the Russian economy. New institutions will be established to assist in the creation of small and medium-size firms, as well as mergers designed to raise productivity. Loss-making firms will be advised to consolidate; once their owners agree to combine, specialized agencies will assist them technologically and financially. The government is already working on a program for "industrial assembly" of the automotive industry. Special economic zones will be established with the express objective of providing an impetus to innovative forms of development. In the first stage there will be six such zones, namely, Moscow, Moscow Region, St. Petersburg, Lipetsk, Tomsk and Tatarstan.
3 A significant new emphasis will be placed on the energy sector, reflecting the fact that the energy markets have become ever more globalized and indivisible.[33] This sector has also become critically interrelated with national economic and strategic security interests with protectionist undertones. President Putin has expressed concern

about this trend. The Russian agenda envisions a non-discriminatory commercial policy that would place all prospective foreign investors on an equal footing. Foreign companies would participate in, among other things, the development of Russian energy reserves and in return Russian companies would invest in the refining capacity and retail fuel sales of their foreign counterparts.

As for the energy security of western Europe and the United States, the agenda included three sets of policies that have already been initiated. First, Russian oil and gas companies, be they government-controlled monopolies or privately owned firms, will be directed to conduct business on economic, market-oriented terms. Second, all former Soviet republics will be charged the same prices for Russian oil and gas as are paid by Western countries. For decades, what Western countries have paid has been determined by prices quoted on world markets. That will now be true of all countries. The abolition of discriminatory pricing will bring Russia into conformity with World Trade Organization (WTO) rules, and its trading will be characterized by disclosure, transparency and fairness. Third, Russian oil and gas companies will be encouraged to form partnerships with Western energy companies. Already, Gazprom – Russia's state-controlled gas monopoly – and two German companies, EON and BASF, have established the North European Gas Pipeline Company. Its express purpose is to bring a larger volume of Siberian gas to Germany and Western Europe via the bottom of the Baltic Sea, bypassing the existing pipelines of Ukraine and Poland. Gazprom holds 51 percent of the venture, with the rest split equally between the two German companies. The German government has considered the building of this additional pipeline indispensable for closing the widening gap between demand and supply of natural gas. With 80 percent of Russia's pipelines running to Western Europe, which imports 25 percent of its gas from Russia, mutual interest in energy security is both long term and paramount. Discussing the matter with Angela Merkel, Chancellor of Germany, President Putin said: "Russia will in future supply Europe with as much energy as the continent requires."[34]

4 The new agenda recognizes that improved control of inflation is an essential requisite for the success of Russia's long-term economic restructuring. The government's target rate of inflation for 2005 was 8.5 percent; the actual rate was 10.9 percent (Appendix I). The aim now is gradually to reduce the CPI to a range of 3–6 percent. A lowered rate of inflation and a more stable price level would induce producers to increase productivity in order to raise profits. It would

also tend to further the agenda's aims of increasing the rate of private saving and investment, conditions conducive to replacing aging equipment, especially in manufacturing, communications and transport. Furthermore, a reduced rate of inflation would enable the CBR to lower its refinancing rate, thereby pushing down the commercial banks' lending rates to enterprises and the mortgage rates for housing construction.

5 A firm objective of the government for the medium and longer terms is to reduce the total tax burden. It now stands at 36.8 percent of GDP. But the lowering of corporate taxes will have to await a reduction in the rate of inflation. President Putin has maintained that the current tax structure is a disincentive to expanding production in many sectors of the economy. As part of the new agenda, he has asserted, "Taxes will go down."[35]

6 The new agenda reflects a shift in emphasis regarding monetary and exchange-rate policy. Technically, the CBR has a choice of objectives: to maintain a stable nominal value of the ruble or to decelerate the rate of inflation. In recent years, the nominal value of the ruble has been quite stable. The large current-account surplus and the shift by Russian citizens from dollar to ruble deposits greatly increased the volume of broad money (M2), rendering it more difficult for the CBR to neutralize the effects of the increasing supply of foreign currency. As a consequence, in 2005, the practically stable nominal value of the ruble, combined with the double-digit rate of inflation, had the effect of raising the real effective value of the ruble by about 10 percent. Thus, the competitiveness of Russia's non-energy exports was adversely affected. If the dangers of "Dutch Disease" are to be averted, Russia's ongoing banking reforms will have to be substantially accelerated so that the CBR can improve its regulation of monetary policy. This would appear to be a necessary condition for the achievement of the agenda's related objective of establishing full and satisfactory convertibility of the ruble in the medium term.

7 Timely access to the WTO, on acceptable terms, is a significant aim of the agenda; membership would provide an international anchor for the required economic policy reforms.

8 Implementation of the agenda is made necessary by critical, historic conditions: Russia is a developing country with a weak economic, political and social infrastructure. These conditions, it is maintained, point to the need for presidential power. To best serve its national interest, in the medium and long terms, the Russian government will, the agenda asserts, follow a policy of "balance" between market-oriented forces and state direction of the economy.

This agenda provides a schema of what Russia needs to do economically to sustain its ongoing transition with rapid growth rates. Understandably, the agenda does not discuss the obstacles within Russia to reforming the economy, though such reform is indispensable to the success of the program. The primary obstacles and ways to overcome them will be discussed in the following chapters.

2 Transitional constraints

A dichotomy has emerged between the executive measures designed to improve the function of Russia's politico-economic institutions and the enforcement procedures of the laws and regulation of the state by certain government agencies. During interviews which the author had with members of the Duma and Russian economists in the summer of 1999 and in the fall of 2003 and 2005, the view that this dichotomy has been intensified by an alarming increase in financial lobbying and bribery by business oligarchs of parliamentary members, political parties, customs officials and the courts was frequently expressed.

Russian economists have expressed deep concern about the remaining weaknesses in the Russian political economy. These weaknesses, if not greatly reduced, cannot but impede the necessary long-term attainment of growth rates higher than those projected by the Russian government and by private experts. The reforms that will be recommended in the conclusion of this study, therefore, are applicable to the following contexts.

Quasi-market economy

Russia is paying a heavy price for a relatively backward and inefficient legal and administrative structure that is obstructing the development of a more fully organized market economy. The market-driven policies promoted by the Putin administration are colliding with the residual elements of the old command system still adhered to by ministries, agencies and members of the civil service. From its early history, Russia was organized as a super-centralized state, and this tendency affects the mentality and attitude of its people. Many ministries continue to function like headquarters for branches of a centralized economy. They direct their efforts at bringing enterprises under their control, both financially and administratively. Unwieldy, with overlapping jurisdictions, cumbersome licensing arrangements and inordinate delays, the bureaucracy inflicts higher transaction costs on enterprises, as a percentage of GDP, than those found in any developed Western country. In an annual address to the Duma, President Putin stated that there were 500,000 complaints about regulatory control and government red tape during one year, three-quarters of them alleging arbitrary administrator behavior. These claims, he continued, "are absolutely well founded."[1]

Regional regulations, even more than laws, operate in a perverse manner. They subsidize unproductive enterprises – often bankrupt companies of the state that are not permitted to die – thereby placing otherwise profit-making firms at a disadvantage. The reasons for this phenomenon are neither simple nor singular. Primarily, they are associated with quasi-market conditions. Many enterprises remain responsible for providing their employees and families with supplementary welfare benefits in multifarious forms, such as cafeteria provisions, rental discounts, educational grants and semi-unemployment payments. Allegedly, these non-wage payments are made to help maintain socio-political stability. In turn, the regional authorities subsidize loss-making enterprises via tax exemptions and reductions in costs of oil, gas, transport and electricity services. Such allocations of regional revenues reduce the supply of capital to more productive enterprises, raising their costs and hindering the more optimal use of resources. The subsidized production of inefficient firms also reduces the output of more efficient ones and deters the entry of new small- and medium-sized companies. To remain in operation, normally productive firms are often impelled to apply for such regional subsidization. Systemically, the process shuns transparency; it intensifies corruption.

Compounding these regional controls in industry are those in agriculture. The regional authorities have considerable autonomy in formulating their agricultural policies. This has been exploited in many regions by the imposition of regional trade barriers. Food reserve programs have been utilized to control prices. Commodity-credit schemes have been used as a form of non-cash public procurement. Subsidies have been channeled to support inefficient farm firms. Tax exemptions, including tolerance of non-payments and arrears, still abound. These practices are, of course, inherently distortional. They impede agricultural restructuring and, in consequence, thwart Russia's need to develop its potential comparative advantage in a modernized agricultural plant.

A systematic investigation needs to identify the essential economic functions to be performed by Russian government ministries and agencies. Russian economists have suggested to the author that the Duma would be well advised to trim federal revenue transfers that are now misused by regional authorities on quasi-market activities. In interviews, prominent members of the Duma have emphasized that such transfers obstruct progress toward a more fully organized market economy.

Quasi-independent judiciary

The history of Russia is a history of distrust in the state. For centuries, the Russian state has been regarded as non-transparent by its citizens. Judicial decision-making institutions have not been independent of the executive or legislative branches of the government. They still are quasi-dependent institutions. President Putin has deplored the situation. He has said that the roles of the courts, the law enforcement agencies and the arbitration councils have changed; they must all now work under the effective authority of the law. But, he emphasized, citizens refuse to understand this fundamental change.

> Why don't we pay judges and law enforcement agents the money that they deserve? Because Soviet ideology governs our consciousness to this day. Remember how we used to think: "Well, a court, what's that? Nothing special. The District Party committee is the body that makes all the decisions. It's important. But what do the judges do? They will do what they are told."
>
> To this day, people think that judges are not important, and that they shouldn't be paid more than the average civil servant.[2]

Since President Putin spoke these words, Russian salaries have risen and conditions of the judiciary have improved. The Federal Assembly and the government have collaborated in passing judicial reforms. Private property rights have been strengthened. Land and labor decrees have been incorporated into the civil code. Laws of inheritance in business, agriculture and family relations have become more definite and secure. Rights of minority shareholders, domestic and foreign, have been legally acknowledged. Intellectual property rights, including patents, titles to movie features and television series, are in the process of being harmonized with standards of the WTO. However, important as these advances have been, their implementation has suffered from systemic political, economic and aforementioned ideological weaknesses.

Salaries of judges, court officials and civil servants remain at abysmally low levels in comparison with comparable occupations or relative to the opportunity cost of specialized training for these positions. Without ubiquitous bribery – "power for favor" – it would be impossible for these indispensable public servants to maintain a standard of living commensurate with their professional status. This state of affairs seriously obstructs the further development of a market-based economy.

Systemic corruption

For centuries under the czars, corruption was part of the fabric of Russian society, a theme often expressed in literature and folklore. In Soviet times, government officials frequently dealt with public property that constitutionally belonged to the people as if it were their own. When President Mikhail Gorbachev introduced partial economic liberalization in the period 1986–1988, the fact that government officials were simultaneously operating as businessmen had the effect of increasing corruption.[3]

Nonetheless, recent Russian research on corruption indicates that bureaucrats began to grow very rich only after Communism had collapsed. After the U.S.S.R. and the Communist Party were dissolved in 1991 and President Yeltsin instituted a new, radical government in January 1992, his economic staff jettisoned the old economic structure, freed most prices and foreign trade and began the process of privatization, which eventually led to the sale of most state enterprises. The transition to capitalism, therefore, was made swiftly. But according to Grigory Yavlinsky, two dogmas shaped much of Russia's economic program in the early and mid-1990s. The first dogma, stemming from Marxist ideology – though often disguised in liberal phraseology – was that "primary accumulation of capital" is always a crime.[4] The second dogma, which stemmed largely from orthodox classical economics, was that the structure of property ownership and the market *automatically* creates adequate political and economic superstructures. As a result of these views, the "loans for shares" schemes – implemented by the Yeltsin regime in 1994–1997 – created a powerful group of business oligarchs that "captured the state." The reformers of the time were convinced that it was unimportant to whom property was distributed as long as it was transferred from the state to private hands.

Many of the key resource-based companies fell into the hands of a small group of businessmen – often government insiders – via rigged auctions. Between 1990 and 1998, proceeds to the Russian government from privatization totaled $7.5 billion, compared with Brazil privatization receipts for a roughly comparable volume of assets of $66.7 billion in the same period. Average GDP in the two countries was similar in these years.[5] The Russian government had previously derived much of its income from the assets that had been sold off at scandalously discounted prices. Not only was the state weakened by reduced revenue, but the distribution of wealth and income had become severely skewed. By 1997, when inflation was also a factor, the Gini coefficient for income distribution in Russia was around 0.5, which was comparable to the level of Colombia or Malaysia.[6]

Russian officials report that, since 2000, about 12 business groups have come to control nearly 60 percent of the Russian economy, probably a larger proportion than they controlled in 1998 and certainly a wider range of economic sectors. According to a comprehensive survey by the World Bank, Russian oligarchs hold, on average, nearly 80 percent of the shares in their companies. The proportion of shares in the hands of the "dominant shareholders" is about 70 percent, even for businesses controlled by the public sector, by foreigners and by other private owners. The leader of the Liberal Democratic Party in the Duma declared that regular payments were made by companies to officials placed by them in various parts of the state apparatus. The stakes of the authorities and greed, he added, associated with the reforms of the 1990s led to the formation of semi-criminal oligarchic business and political life.[7] In a survey of 7,504 citizens, it was found that businessmen paid $33 billion in bribes, equal to nearly half of the federal budget revenues in 2002. Other citizens paid about $3 billion in bribes annually, about half of what they paid in income taxes. At least one-third of the deputies in the Duma owned their businesses.[8] Marked by immense industrial concentration, Russian companies lack checks and balances, either from diversified stockholders on their boards or from external controls.[9]

It is the coalescence of business and government that has been largely responsible for generating these conditions. President Putin has not underestimated the seriousness of the problem:

> I would like to note that the way the state is organized at present unfortunately promotes corruption. It is not that we are not trying to clamp down on it. I would like to stress that corruption is a direct consequence of the restrictions on freedoms. The higher the barrier, the greater the bribe and the more highly placed the official taking it.[10]

In mid-May 2006, President Putin accused Russian officials of smuggling cars, wine and even yachts to Russia and of skimming billions of dollars in duties. At a cabinet meeting about a month earlier, which was broadcast on state television, he asked the Minister of Trade and Economic Development when he was going to stop the practice of customs units and businessmen merging in economic ecstasy at most of the border crossings. On May 11, he took action against bureaucratic corruption. First, he transferred the Customs Service – a lucrative prize in Russian politics – from the control of the Minister of Trade and Economic Development to direct oversight by the prime minister. Senior officials in the Customs Service had allied themselves to two senators who were now placed on recall. Then, on May 12, the president fired the head of the Customs Service and about a dozen of his subordinates. Among other officials fired were three deputy heads of the Federal Security Service, four senior criminal investigators in the Internal Ministry and two deputies in the powerful General Prosecutor's Office. At the president's request, on June 3, 2006, the parliament dismissed the prosecutor-general, Vladimir Ustinov, who had been appointed by President Yeltsin and had served since 2000.[11]

Following these events, the chairman of a notable research group in Moscow, the National Strategy Institute, said, "We don't see any struggle against corruption as a *matter of policy*. This is competition in the system and level of influence."[12] The view relates to an important controversial issue: what it would take to effectively implement edicts and/or reforms against corruption. In Russia, it is often argued, strategic location and strength of domestic interest groups could readily frustrate anticorruption measures or economic reforms. Accordingly, these weaknesses within Russia could distort reforms in the course of implementation. A critical issue, therefore, is the content of the enabling legislation that follows changes in the edicts or the laws. If officials within the state bureaucracy want to frustrate the intended effects of legal changes, they need only influence the content of enabling legislation. Doubtless, such obstacles to reforms are widespread in Russia. A definitive analysis of them awaits its historian. But these conditions are not necessarily inconsistent with the struggle against corruptions as a "matter of policy." An important policy reform in Russia is to establish, implement and sustain essential changes in economic regulations and laws.

Some Russian scholars have also argued that corruption is not an inextricable part of the Russian character or culture; they maintain that it is a curable phenomenon resulting primarily from systemic causes. This, of course, is an exaggeration; history, character and opportunity cost clearly have also had their effect.[13] As for policy measures to reduce systemic corruption, specific recommendations are made in the conclusion of this study regarding the conflicts between the key groups – the executive, parliament, judicial system and the business community. Reducing these conflicts, it will be argued, is contingent on bringing about a greater degree of compliance with respect to the basic principles of a competitive market-oriented economy. A key issue is whether Russian and American leaders will be tempted to pursue short-term policies, respectively, of the (1) "petro-assertive" and (2) "hawkish-protectionist" variety, or long-term policies of more enlightened, open globalization. The following brief sketch of President Putin's career may provide some insight into his probable approach to the issues at hand.

Box 2.1

Vladimir V. Putin

Born on October 8, 1952, in St. Peterburg – then Leningrad – Putin was raised in a humble, well-disciplined family. As a young man he was inspired by his mother to succeed in worthy pursuits and to gain respect from more robust peers. An excellent senior student, Putin graduated from the State University of Leningrad faculty of law in 1974. From 1975 to 1990, he served with the Soviet security services in the intelligence branch (KGB). He resigned from that post in 1990 and joined the staff of Anatoly A. Sobchak, mayor of St. Petersburg, who had been one of his professors and subsequently a mentor. In 1991, Putin was appointed assistant rector of international affairs in the Leningrad State University. From March 1994 to July 1996, he served as deputy mayor of St. Petersburg. Then he left for Moscow to serve on the staff of President Boris N. Yeltsin. Concurrently, in 1996, Putin became a candidate in Economic Sciences. In 1998, Yeltsin made Putin his deputy chief of staff to serve as head of the powerful Security Council. Though comparatively unknown to the general public, in August 1999 Yeltsin named Putin prime minister. And when Yeltsin resigned as president on December 31, 1999, he appointed Putin acting president. In elections held on March 26, 2000, Putin was elected president with 52.9 percent of the votes. His approval rating in January 2001 was 70 percent, and after the Moscow Theater hostage operation of October 26, 2002, it rose to 77 percent. On March 14, 2004, he was elected for a second term by 70.5 percent of the voters. Setbacks have occurred, however, and his approval ratings have been affected by negative reactions at home and abroad. According to the independent Levada Center in Moscow, approval declined to about 65 percent in the early months of 2005, but by March 2006 had risen again to 72 percent.

Analytical, pragmatic, iron-willed patriot – although legalistic – when, early in his presidency, Putin was asked what the requirements were for a Code to achieve Russia's needs and goals, he replied, "Moral values."[1]

However, the Yukos crisis (described in Chapter 5) and the following events have adversely affected Putin's image in Western countries.

- On September 13, 2004, he proposed, and the Duma enacted, legislation disallowing the election by popular vote of governors and leaders of the country's 89 regions.
- Before the Ukraine presidential election of November 21, 2004, Putin publicly supported the candidacy of Prime Minister Victor F. Yanukovich. Yanukovich headed an administration that had been excoriated by independent observers for corruption and massive electrol fraud.
- On January 1, 2006, in a dispute with Ukraine over its refusal to accept Russia's decision to raise the price of gas so that it would be more closely aligned with world market levels, Russia cut off Ukraine's gas supply. But since the pipeline ran through Ukraine to western Europe, Ukraine was able to tap a considerable volume of gas intended for western European countries. This development raised an alarm across the continent about the reliability of Russia as a supplier of energy.
- On March 19, 2006, Aleksandr G. Lukashenko was elected president of Belarus for a third five-year term, allegedly with 82.6 percent of the vote. The governments of western Europe and the United States accused him of electoral fraud and violent crackdowns on dissent. They unanimously condemned the election, while Putin supported it.

At his annual news conference with international journalists on January 31, 2006, Putin endeavored to clarify his decisions on most of these aforementioned issues. Indeed, as will be shown, he appears to have modified his views on some of them.

A foreign journalist asked Putin a seemingly lighthearted question that brought forth an unexpected weighty response. What was the meaning of judo to Putin? As a sport, he replied, he enjoyed it very much, but it was also a facet of world culture. Judo's slogan, he said, was "harmony with the world around us and with ourselves."[2] This was an important philosophical premise, he continued, for it was key to attaining a goal in any sphere. Furthermore, courage combined with nobleness was a distinguishing feature of judo's combat. "We, in Russia," he vowed, "will do everything possible in accordance with these principles, both in politics and in sport."[3]

Putin concluded the conference by answering a question about the right to choose. Freedom and the right to choose, he asserted, are basic values: "If we can ensure these in society, it will be a great accomplishment for us."[4] Manifestly, these views are applicable not only to Russia but to the former Soviet republics as well.

Notes

1 Vladimir V. Putin, *First Person* (New York: Public Affairs 2001), p. 161; See also pp. 174–196. For further bibliographical material, see the instructive interviews in this publication and the excellent book by Oleg Blotskii, *Vladimir Putin, Istorria Zhizni (The History of a Life. Prima Facie)*, vol 1, 1952–1974 (Moscow: Mezhdunarodnye Otnosheniia, 2001); Peter Truscott, *Putin's Progress. A Bibliography of Russia's Enigmatic President* (New York: Simon & Schuster, 2004).
2 "Original Text of Putin's Annual News Conference for International Journalists," BBC Monitoring, Moscow, January 31, 2006, pp. 28–29.
3 Op. cit. *BBC Monitoring*, pp. 48–49
4 Ibid.

3 Basic principles toward a successful Russian market economy

In a free-market economy, not only do output and wealth creation reflect the value preferences of the people, but these preferences, in turn, are reflected in the market signals. A key aspect of a successful market system is that the value of any physical production facility depends on the perceived value of the goods and services that the facility is projected to produce.[1] Technically, the current value of the facility is the sum of the discounted value of all future outputs, net of costs. The value of the facility thus depends on how investors view the markets into which the output of the facility would be sold and on profitability. However, profitability will depend not only on such factors as the competence of management, the level of interest rates, the overall rate of inflation and the degree of mutual trust between sellers and buyers, but also on the extent of collusion and corruption among businessmen and officials in manipulating markets.

Hence, a fundamental economic concept is that, per se, natural and human resources as well as plant, equipment and even markets have no intrinsic economic value: they are only valuable if they can satisfy needs currently or are perceived to be able to satisfy needs in the future. Resources closely tied to technology, education, training or organization that are obsolete may be unable to produce goods and services that have current or future value. Russia's abundance of natural and human resources, therefore, may become a pillar of its future progress, but only if they are to embrace these values. A key problem is not how to preserve the value of Russia's existing natural and human resources, but how to give value to its *potential* natural capital. In most sectors, this will require the continuation of serious reforms, large investments and much restructuring. The preceding comments on necessary conditions for the success of a market economy point to measures that appear to be essential for these developments.

Regarding the relations between scientists, engineers and market forces, scholars have long recognized that an innovation's full *potential* may be realized only after extensive improvements or after complementary innovations in other fields of science. According to my colleague Charles H. Townes, Nobel Prize winner for his work on the laser, "An attorney for Bell Labs, in 1958, initially declined to patent the laser because he felt it had no simple application in the field of communications."[2] But Townes was able to convince the lawyer by describing a simple system that would employ a laser. The modern importance of lasers in telecommunications became clear only after the scientific and technical community had developed excellent lasers and low-loss fiber optics over the following decade. As the Russian Nobel Laureate Zh. I. Alferov observed, it is hardly possible to imagine our recent life without laser-based telecommunication systems, including satellite televisions, space and terrestrial applications.[3] John R. Whinnery has noted, "From an economic point of view, costs will decrease dramatically as use increases, as has been demonstrated by lasers used with compact disc (CD) players."[4]

There has been a fundamental difference between the "economic cultures" of Russia and developed Western countries in regard to scientific research and its commercial application. In the United States, for example, disregarding fluctuations associated with the business cycle, the application of scientific breakthroughs and newly discovered engineering technologies to civilian commercial ends has been quite continuous and often spectacular since World War II. The process of profit maximization in this regard is extremely difficult as it entails smoothing application of technologies from one period to another. But this, of course, has not curtailed large expenditures on research and development.[5] American managers generally stay abreast of the work being done in the major labs and in the universities, and they frequently maintain contact with those involved in research. They thus serve as intermediaries between the scientific community and the market place. In Russia, a weak "economic culture" inhibits this kind of activity in the non-military sphere, which helps to account for the extremely slow diversification of Russia's non-natural-resource production structure.

During the last two decades, in particular, the connection between significant technological and scientific advances and periods of robust economic growth has been manifest in the United States. "Creative destruction" was often combined with innovative human protection via new safety nets. For instance, the substitution of transistors for vacuum tubes dramatically reduced the size of radios and generalized the economies of size and space. The fiber-optic cable has replaced the huge tonnage of copper. New architectural engineering and new materials' technologies have enabled the construction of building with far less physical materials. As a result, the physical weight of U.S. GDP has been growing very gradually.

The expansions of new technical concepts account for virtually all of the inflation-adjusted growth in output. More generally, as technological frontiers were moved forward and faster information processing became necessary, the laws of physics required evermore compact microchips. Such advances are dependent not only on the high investment in research and development but also on continuous dialog between scientists and entrepreneurs. Such dialog is growing in Russia, but it is still quite infrequent. Similarly, investment by government and private firms in research and development is extremely low.[6] These deficiencies will have to be corrected if President Putin's ambitious objective of doubling Russia's GDP in a decade – a quantum jump in average GDP growth rates of 7 to 8 percent – is to be achieved.

4 Policy reforms for the longer term

(1) This study has identified three phases of Russia's economic transition during the period from late 1998 to 2005 that appear to have provided the foundations for its longer-term economic diversification, Western integration and policy reform. To conduct the analysis, a series was derived of Russia's real GDP in terms of the U.S. dollar for 1989–2005. It was shown that, in the first phase, economic recovery occurred principally as a result of elimination of an overvalued exchange rate of the ruble with respect to the non-energy sectors following the financial crisis of August 1998. The evidence indicates that the energy sector was insignificant in the first phase of the economic transition. The real depreciation of the ruble had the effect of bringing Russia's cost-price structures in agriculture and in the non-energy industries in line with international competitive conditions. Though some promising economic diversification had occurred, in the absence of significant structural and banking reforms it was in the order of "second smalls." The evidence of the first transition phase is relevant for the longer term: Russia's huge comparative advantage in the oil and gas industries tends to overvalue the ruble in terms of most other sectors, hindering the rate of growth and the pace of economic diversification. It is difficult to overestimate the importance of pursuing economic policies that will check the inherent tendency of the ruble to become overvalued with respect to the bulk of Russia's internationally traded non-energy exports.

(2) The second phase of the transition was marked by high world energy prices. Nevertheless, during this phase, even a moderate decline in the price of oil demonstrated the immense effect of this sector on Russia's external accounts and on the budget balance. Given the volatility of world oil prices and Russia's fledgling correlation with the international economy, the analysis in this study points to the need for a two-pronged approach to Russia's macroeconomic policies. For the next few years, experience suggests that a "restrained" fiscal policy – an average budget surplus during the business cycle of about 2.5 percent of GDP – would

contribute to the achievement of robust growth rates via a further lowering of inter-rate spreads in international financial markets, a reduction in the foreign debt to GDP ratio and a raising of Russia's debt ratings to "investment grade" for both sovereign and corporate investments (see Appendix I). For the short term, Russia requires financial institutions that would stimulate the economy rapidly in times of substantially declining growth rates associated with such factors as cyclical contraction and/or plummeting world oil prices, allowing the budget surplus to decline or even to move into a moderate budget deficit. But, unfortunately, Russia does not yet have the necessary instruments to implement these tasks. It is caught in an institutional trap: the banking system has not been sufficiently reformed and the tax structure is not sufficiently broad to provide the necessary transition mechanisms for economic resilience. *Inter alia*, the operation of an independent, economically managed oil stabilization fund to assist in maintaining fiscal balance and in raising Russia's long-term GDP growth rate could contribute to achieving the preceding objectives.[1] A portion of government revenues derived from oil should annually be allocated to the fund for the express purpose of investing these funds in diversified, major foreign-government securities. These funds would grow as long as the world price of oil was above a designated moving-average norm. When the price of oil fell significantly below this level, the authority would sell an appropriate volume of foreign securities and transfer the proceeds to the Ministry of Finance, thereby contributing to fiscal balance.[2] In the long term, the net purchase of foreign securities by the fund would also contribute to dampen the tendency of the ruble to become overvalued.

(3) During the third phase of the economic transition, Russia experienced significant economic successes, ranging from increasing profitability and the slashing of payment arrears to rising per capita income and improved macro- and microeconomic management (Figures 1.5–1.7). Though these advances began before President Putin's first term in office, they steadily progressed under his leadership to provide political-economic stability. However, the banking system was neither reformed nor restructured. The economic advance effectively masked this failure. The conventional wisdom that Russia would be unable to experience a successful economic transition without a restructuring of its banking system was erroneous. Economic analysis and historic experience indicate, however, that in the longer term, if a weak banking system is not reformed, a subsequent economic decline is likely to degenerate into a period of stagnation. By early 2002, the importance of granting the CBR greater independence in conducting monetary policy had become manifest. President Putin appointed a new, professional team with the express objective of making the bank more independent from both the Duma and the

executive branch of the government. This would provide the necessary institutional foundation and mechanism for more rapid progress in restructuring the banking system. In accordance with President Putin's new economic agenda, it would also assist in establishing external convertibility of the ruble.[3] However, its sustainability is in question. Powerful members of the Duma believe that higher levels of inflation are less serious for the economy than forgoing other national priorities. They are likely to undermine the Bank's anti-inflationary efforts. Rising wages relative to rising labor productivity are rendering it more difficult to lower the CPI (Figure II.1). It is difficult to overestimate the importance of the executive holding the Duma – and the CBR – to the state inflationary targets.

(4) There are compelling reasons for establishing equality of treatment in the banking industry. Deposit insurance, which until recently has been provided primarily by the government-owned Sberbank, should be generalized for all Russian commercial banks on equal non-subsidized terms. The gradual reform of utility pricing in oil, gas and housing urgently requires the development of a modern mortgage-investment sector in order to increase investment in affordable housing, to raise household capitalization and to help increase labor mobility. While Russian conditions of severe poverty demand official, standard assistance in health and education, extra quality provisions must be met by personal payments.

(5) The anemic state of the world economy in the second half of 2002 adversely affected Russia's GDP growth rate; it declined from 5 percent in 2001 to 4.6 percent in 2002, while the rate of increase of fixed capital formation fell from 8.7 to 2.6 percent and the rate of change of capacity utilization from 8.8 to 0.9 percent. But the first half of 2003 witnessed a buoyant turnaround in Russia's economy: GDP growth for the year rose to 7.3 percent, the rate of increase of fixed capital formation rose to 12.2 percent and the rate of change of capacity utilization rose to 4.7 percent.[4] This was associated with high world energy prices, increased domestic energy production and a construction boom. Russia's current-account surplus surged. Foreign exchange reserves grew rapidly. On February 17, 2003, the CBR lowered its refinancing rate and the overnight inter-bank loan rate was reduced to 1–2 percent: the entire structure of real interest rates fell. The demand for and the supply of practically all monetary instruments rose. Credence in Russia's economic stabilization and potential long-term economic advance was becoming ever more manifest. A string of bonds were issued on both domestic and international financial markets. The yield on Russia's short-term government securities declined to single-digit levels. Comparable declines were registered for equities of large oil companies.[5] As noted, British Petroleum concluded a landmark merger with Russia's TNK oil group, and major American oil companies

entered into negotiations with Yukos, Russia's largest oil company at the time, for even larger deals.[6] Gazprom, Russia's government-controlled giant gas monopoly, reported one of its best first-half results of the past decade.[7] By July 2003, the CBR's foreign exchange reserves had reached record levels of more than $60 billion. For the first time since the collapse of Communism, Russia experienced a substantial net inflow of private capital. In early October, Moody's Investors Services upgraded Russia's sovereign bonds to "investment grade."[8]

This positive economic climate was shattered by the actions of the prosecutor-general's office in arresting the head of Yukos on October 25 and freezing his dominant stake in Yukos on October 30 (see Chapter 5, infra). These events generated abroad an image of selective justice, arbitrariness and zealousness.[9] In protest, President Putin's chief of staff resigned.[10] The financial community was beset by uncertainty. Negotiations on mergers between Yukos and major American oil companies came to a halt. For the week following the chief executive's arrest, Russia's Trading System (RTS) index fell by 16.5 percent; the price of Yukos share plunged by one-third.[11] Government officials feared that, once again, capital flight would be resumed.[12] On November 3, 2003, the chief executive of Yukos resigned and transferred control of his stocks to another shareholder while he was incarcerated. In a determined effort, President Putin and his key ministers launched a campaign to quell the financial crisis. Addressing the Russian Union of Industrialists and Entrepreneurs, the president asked rhetorically:

> Will there be a return to the past? There will not. The state must prosecute criminals, but it must also protect everybody, including and not least of all business, because that means protecting the economy of the state.[13]

He had no intention of revisiting the privatization of the 1990s. As for Yukos, there was no intention to launch a general crack down on the circle of billionaires: "The state surely does not want to destroy the company," said Putin.[14] He stressed, however, that he would not let businessmen run the state and that there must be a dividing line between business and the authorities. After the president's reportedly "dazzling" presentation, domestic financial markets stabilized and foreign investment in Russia continued apace. But the zealous way in which the prosecutor-general's office had handled the Yukos affair was dysfunctional and counterproductive; much avoidable damage had been done both at home and abroad to the credibility and predictability of the Russian political economy, following a period in which both had reached new highs. On March 14, 2004,

Putin was re-elected president with a 70.5 percent share of the vote. However, setbacks in the economy occurred in the following months. Despite record-high world prices for oil and gas, the annualized GDP growth rate decelerated from about 7.7 percent in 2003 to 6.7 percent in 2004, and official projections for 2004 predicted a further deceleration to 6.6 percent. The general slowdown appears to have been associated largely with increased business anxiety about the new administration's policies on historic taxation claims, on property rights and on government control of strategic economic sectors.

(6) The evolutionary task of coordinating Russia's economic interest – via a more fully fledged competitive market system – with the country's political and legal systems would be enhanced by assistance from the United States and key western European countries in further integrating Russia with the norms and practices of major international economic organizations. Russia's accession to the WTO could make a significant contribution to the attainment of these objectives. It would be not only an important step in the country's integration with the European Atlantic Community, but also an even greater step in joining the world community. President Putin has spoken of a "vision" of Russia intertwined with western Europe economically, socially and politically: "By their mentality and culture", he has maintained, "the people of Russia are European."[15] Chancellor Kohl assured him that he could not imagine a Europe without Russia. Furthermore, the chancellor declared that the Germans "were not only interested in the Russian market but in becoming worthy partners with Russia."[16] As for the United States, President George H.W. Bush, in referring to the revolutionary times in which he was in office (1989–1993), expressed the permanent American interest in a healthy Russian economy.[17] The United States, he wrote, has a continuous and abiding concern about international security. At present, this centers on such issues as collaboration on the war against international terrorism, the cessation of production and proliferation of non-conventional weapons by adversaries and the supply of strategic raw materials. An expansion of foreign trade and investment clearly would serve their interdependent national interests.

(7) The global proportions of Russia's GDP, foreign trade and investment are still extremely small, impeding its influence on and benefits from key international economic institutions.[18] An analysis by the EBRD of 83 countries around the world has shown that Russia has been trading much less than theoretical models would predict.[19] The introduction into the analysis of an index, developed by the World Bank, that incorporates such factors as institutional and administrative constraints – e.g., regional trade barriers, high transaction costs associated with licensing and customs delays and corruption – throws much light on Russia's comparatively

small volume of foreign trade. Commitment to reforms that would reduce many of these constraints, which is standard requirement for accession to the WTO, would most likely increase Russia's share of international trade and global GDP.[20]

(8) As a member of the WTO, Russia would be in a better position to diversify and to expand its production and foreign trade, for according to the "new international economics," the bulk of international trade is determined by comparative advantage and trade in differentiated products, by economies of scale and by advantages in imperfect competition.[21] Well endowed with scientists, engineers and mathematicians, as well as with a low-cost, highly motivated young labor force, Russia appears to have good potentialities in these respects.[22] The diversification of the economy would tend to contribute to the rate of growth in international trade and to mitigate the impact of external cyclical and oil shocks.

(9) Accessions to membership in the WTO would require comprehensive commitments by the Russian government to reduce its tariff schedules and to provide greater "market access" to all of its regions. The implementation of these commitments in the medium term, prescribed by WTO rules and regulations, would increase long-term economic flexibility within and among the interregional sectors. Tribunals would be established for the prompt review of trade and investment procedures. Moreover, usually within one year, independent and impartial tribunals would provide decisions on commercial disputes. The mutual advantages to the 151 WTO member states (including Russia) would be incorporated in key provisions of General Agreement Terms in Trade and Services (GATS), tariff quotas (TRQs) and Trade-Related Intellectual Property Rights (TRIPs), as well as in agreements on foreign investment, telecommunications and the opening of distribution facilities in Russia's domestic markets. The commitments made under the GATS would be legally binding and reflected in regulations at the central, regional and local levels of Russian government. In effect, this would build a body of commercial law in Russia conforming to WTO standards and would foster interdependence between external and internal codes.

Freer trade, per se, ensures neither robust GDP growth rates nor reductions in grinding poverty, nor compliance with negotiated trade terms. The last, in Russia, would require the above-identified structural reforms and policies focused on reducing the endemic poverty of some 22 million people still living below the minimum poverty line.

5 The Yukos crisis

In early February 2000, President Putin struck a deal with Russia's business oligarchs: if they did not try to run the government, paid their taxes and invested in Russia, they would be allowed to keep the fortunes they had acquired by shrewd but non-criminal means via the privatization schemes of the 1990s. Yukos, Russia's largest oil company at the time, whose chief executive, Mikhail Khodorkovsky, was also Russia's richest man, followed a policy of exploiting existing oil supplies, rather than investing in new exploration. The company also used offshore regions, such as Armenia and Moldova, to ship oil abroad; these were regions that offered Yukos low or zero tax rates. Consequently, in 2000, Yukos' corporate income-tax rate was under 20 percent, compared with a statutory rate of 24 percent in Russia.[1] This situation continued from 2000 to mid-2003.

The state prosecutor-general, on July 2, 2003, launched an attack on the central offices of Yukos. Armed and masked, the police stormed the building and in their assault arrested the main security officer, Aleksei Pichugin, and one of Yukos' main shareholders, Platon Lebedev. The prosecutor-general charged that Yukos was suspected of murderous acts, theft and tax evasion in privatization deals dating back to 1994.[2] Russia's most respected human-rights organization condemned the repressive measures used by the prosecutor-general's office.

In response to allegations in the public media that the attack against Yukos was politically motivated, President Putin's spokesman declared that the president had not initiated the attack. In fact, he condemned it. Moreover, he had not even been consulted on the matter. Publicly, he had tried not to take sides in the conflict. Putin explained, qua president he could not simply tell prosecutors to stop investigating suspected crimes. Nonetheless, he had sent "all the necessary signals that their actions were hurting the political and economic situation in the country."[3] The president and the foreign minister made it clear that they had no intention of reviewing the origins of fortunes made in the privatization deals of the 1990s.

Much damage had been done by the attack on Yukos. Share prices plunged, and capital flight from the end of May to September amounted to $2.8 billion contributing to a decline of 4.5 percent in the foreign exchange reserves of Russia's central bank.[4] Still, by the end of July 2003, when signs appeared of a resolution to the conflict involving the prosecutor-general, Yukos and the Kremlin, major American oil companies resumed their plans to make large investments in Yukos.[5] These plans appeared reasonable, for although Khodorkovsky had maintained that the prosecutor's investigations were triggered by his company's decision in the spring of 2003 to merge with its major rival Sibneft, Russia's antimonopoly ministry gave formal approval to the merger in August 2003. The new group was to be called Yukos-Sibneft Oil Company and would have been the world's fourth largest oil producer.

However, a member of the State Duma petitioned the prosecutor-general to investigate the financial history of the Yukos group. After an intensive investigation, on October 17, 2003, Khodorkovsky's holding company – Menatep, which controlled more than 60 percent of Yukos' shares – was charged with tax evasion. Shortly thereafter, on October 25, masked security agents arrested Khodorkovsky on board his private jet during a fuel layover in Siberia. He, then, was charged with tax evasion, embezzlement and fraud. Taken back to Moscow, he was imprisoned and a judge approved his transfer to a pre-trial detention center. Further, on October 30, the prosecutor-general's office impounded 40 percent of Yukos' shares, allegedly as pre-emptive collateral on the company's unpaid taxes for the financial year 2000.

Khodorkovsky was the major owner of the total Yukos' shares, 44 percent of the total. The charges against him and those against Yukos were therefore interrelated. On November 3, 2003, Khodorkovsky resigned his post as chief executive of Yukos and transferred control of his stock to another key shareholder, Leonid Nevzlin, for the period of his incarceration. The Sibneft Company, on November 29, suspended the long-planned merger with Yukos, which technically had been completed in October.[6]

Separately, seven charges were brought by the state authorities against Khodorkovsky as an individual. To wit: when Apatit, a catalytic fertilizer manufacturing company, was privatized in 1994, he and Lebedev had acquired that company via manipulated bidding. Through one of Menatep's affiliates, Volna, they had bid for a 20 percent stake in Apatit after engineering the withdrawal of higher bids. As part of the purchase, Volna had made a commitment to invest $280 million for the modernization of Apatit, but failed to deliver on its pledge. This default led Russia's Federal Property Fund to contest Volna's ownership of Apatit. Following murky negotiations, the fund released Volna from its commitment but required the company to add $15 million to the price it had paid for Apatit. Though this suspect arrangement was subsequently investigated, the prosecutor-general's office found no ground for legal action against Volna. However, several months later, the case was reopened on grounds of "changed conditions" and a Moscow court, in a preliminary ruling, brought charges of fraud and theft of state property amounting to about one billion dollars against Khodorkovsky.[7]

Yukos' shares had been sold in international financial markets to a larger extent than any other Russian corporate security. Since the rule of law in Russia is still often subservient to politics, investors had expressed concern that the Kremlin might sell Yukos' assets at discounted prices and force the company into bankruptcy. Supporters of Yukos have fought their case in the court of public opinion – especially in the West. Whatever the Kremlin's motivations may be, the source of the Yukos crisis lies in the evolutionary conflict between the legal process of eradicating extreme corruption and the government's assurance of property rights essential for a successful, free market economy.

The strained relations between prosecutors, business and the Kremlin turned a commercial and legal conflict into a national financial crisis.[8] In March 2004, a Moscow court barred Yukos from selling any of its assets except crude oil. In June 2004, Russia's tax ministry won a series of court rulings endorsing its claim that Yukos underpaid $3.4 billion in taxes for the 2000 financial year. The company and Khodorkovsky sent several proposals to the prime minister and to the finance minister suggesting terms for an out-of-court settlement of the claim, but the Kremlin declared that a settlement could be reached only in the courts. Yukos then failed to meet a July 7 payment deadline set by a Moscow court. On July 20, 2004, the Justice Ministry announced its intention to sell Yukos' major production unit, Yuganskneftegaz (Yugansk), which accounted for about 60 percent of total Yukos oil production.[9] Investor concern about Yukos' solvency led to a crash in the value of the company's shares. Russia's RTS index, as well as the price of Russia's bonds in international markets, declined. Moreover, Russia's central bank reported a net outflow of capital amounting to $5.5 billion for the first half of 2004, as compared with an inflow of $2.9 billion for the same period for 2003. Despite President Putin's high popularity and the strong condition of the Russian economy, the Deutsche Bank Eurasia group's Stability Index for Russia, measuring the country's ability to avert and withstand crises, fell from 60 to 57 in the year ending June 30, 2004.

Events in the second half of the year exacerbated the Yukos crisis. The Tax Ministry issued claims amounting to $21 billion against the company for unpaid taxes and penalties in the period 2000–2003. Additional claims were issued against the company's subsidiaries – principally against Yugansk – increasing the tax liabilities of the consolidated group to $27.5 billion. Yukos protested, arguing that the additional claims aimed at lowering the market value of the subsidiaries for the express purpose of selling them to government-backed companies and, thereby, helping to settle the tax claims of Yukos itself.[10] On November 3, Yukos announced that an extraordinary meeting of shareholders would take place on December 20 to liquidate the company or to file for bankruptcy protection.[11] In the prevailing economic and political climate, this development had weighty implications. The government was already struggling to reconcile the further opening of its economy with the protection of its strategic energy sector from foreign control. To this end, a merger had been initiated between state-backed Gazprom and state-owned Rosneft Oil Company that was to give the government at least 50 percent plus one share control in the integrated Gazprom group while enabling President Putin to keep his promise to lift restrictions on foreign purchases of Gazprom stock. Yukos was not the asset, in the view of the government, that needed to be secured for Russia.[12] On November 29, the State Property Fund announced an auction of Yugansk on December 19.[13] One day later, Gazprom said it would participate in the auction.[14]

However, on December 16, the Bankruptcy Court in Houston, Texas, granted a request from Yukos for a ten-day restraining order prohibiting the sale of Yugansk to Gazprom or any of its affiliates. The court order applied as well to any bank that might assist in financing such a transaction.[15] Indeed, a syndicate of banks headed by Deutsche Bank and including J.P. Morgan had pledged a $13.2 billion loan to Gazprom for this purpose. But the banks were warned by their lawyers that any move to defy the court order would put their U.S. banking licenses at risk. The syndicate withdrew its pledge.[16] Only two parties submitted the required $1.7 billion deposit to participate in the auction. One was a registered entity in the town of Tver, situated 170 miles northwest of Moscow, which was said to be unknown to the government.[17] Although the initial bidding price was set by the government at a low level of $8.65 billion, Gazprom made no bid whatsoever. Baikal Finance group purchased 76.6 percent of Yugansk shares for $9.35 billion.[18]

When Russia's finance minister, Alexei Kudrin, was asked about Baikal, he said he had never heard of the group.[19] Neither had the press. President Putin, however, did know Baikal. He told German interviewers: "The shareholders of that company are exclusively private individuals who for many years have engaged in the energy business. As far as I know, they intend to establish certain relationships with other energy companies which may be interested in the asset."[20] As far as he understood and was informed, he said, the sale of Yugansk shares was conducted in strict accordance with Russian legislation.

On December 22, Rosneft purchased Baikal in its entirety, but would not disclose the price.[21] Yukos then asserted that whoever had sold, bought or financed the purchase of Yugansk stock, be it through direct or indirect transactions, had violated state law, whether or not they had been named in the American court's order. Furthermore, Yukos would file a $20 billion claim for damages against the Russian government and others involved in the forced auction.[22] In an attempt to protect themselves against lawsuits, Gazprom and Rosneft announced that they were considering a transfer of the Yugansk shares to a new government-owned entity created for the purpose.[23] On February 24, 2005, the Houston Federal Bankruptcy Court dismissed the Yukos filing for bankruptcy protection under American law, thereby removing the legal barriers for the merger of Gazprom and Rosneft.[24] But Rosneft preferred to remain independent and, in May 2005, the Russian government scrapped plans for the merger. A month later, it purchased 10.7 percent of Gazprom's shares, lifting its stake in the company to 50 percent plus one share, thereby paving the way for foreigners to purchase Gazprom shares in the Russian domestic market.[25]

However, controversy continued over the Yugansk auction. On October 24, 2005, a group of U.S. holders of Yukos American depository receipts (ADRs) filed a civil lawsuit in a Washington district court against the Russian government – including Gazprom and Rosneft – claiming that the parties had conspired to renationalize Yukos without compensating the owners.[26] If this lawsuit is successful, it would open the floodgates for claims by other American, as well as European, stockholders of Yukos ADRs.

Before the Yugansk auction, a group of Western bankers led by Société Générale extended a loan of $482 million to Yukos. In a murky negotiation, the banks filed bankruptcy procedures in a Moscow court against Yukos, and later Rosneft purchased the Yukos debt from the banks.[27] Yukos, therefore, became legally indebted to Rosneft. On March 28, 2006, a Moscow court put Yukos under "external supervision," declaring that the managers of Yukos, many of whom were Americans stationed in London, could remain at their jobs, but any important decisions would have to be approved by the external supervisor.[28] Furthermore, for many years, Yukos had a majority stake in the largest oil refinery in Lithuania, Mazeikiu Nafta. In April 2006, the managers of Yukos were completing negotiations with Lithuanian authorities on the expressed purpose of reselling Yukos' shares to the Lithuanian government. Yukos had announced that it planned to use the proceeds from the sale to repay a $600 million debt to Menatep, the majority shareholder of Yukos, still controlled by Mr. Khodorkovsky's associates. But the prevailing U.S. court injunction was designed to block any sale of Yukos' assets. The Lithuanian government resolutely expressed its concern that a Russian state-controlled company, e.g. Gazprom or Rosneft, would attempt to attain majority control over Mazeikiu. Some Lithuanian officials even admonished that increased economic dependence on energy supplies in Russia would endanger the country's political independence. Though they acknowledged that Russian oil companies had met their contractual obligations, Lithuania would, nonetheless, plan to diversify its sources of supply.[29] The U.S. court injunction blocking the sale of Yukos' assets was revoked and the Lithuanian government solicited a major Polish refinery, Orlen, to acquire Mazeikiu. Manifestly, the Yukos crisis, combined with the Russia–Ukraine gas controversy, had intensified distrust and conflict between former Soviet republics in Europe and Russia.

As in all significant economic phenomena, the effects of the Yukos crisis are likely to be substantially different in the short and medium terms than in the long term. Thus, the process of dismantling Yukos generated not only huge losses in the Russian economy but also much discord with Western countries. As the company's tax liabilities from September 2003 to November 2004 ballooned, its bankruptcy was endangered and the value of its shares fell by 93 percent. The general business climate became more and more uncertain, and with each development in the crisis, the Moscow RTS Stock Exchange Index plummeted further. In March 2004, the index was at 752.7; in July, it was at 540.3 (Figure 1.9). Heavy capital flight resumed. Net capital outflows from the non-banking sector rose from $0.8 billion in the first quarter of 2004 to $2.9 billion in the second quarter and to $8.9 billion in the third quarter.[30] The rate of growth in investment and in many industrial sectors declined, lowering the annual GDP growth rate despite the fact that world prices of oil and gas were at extraordinarily high levels. Moreover, official data indicate that Russia experienced a marked economic slowdown between mid-2003 and the end of the third quarter of 2004 (Figure 1.3). The economy appeared to be stabilizing in the fourth quarter of 2004, but on a year-on-year basis, its rate of growth decelerated in the first quarter of 2005 to about 5.2 percent – the lowest rate in almost three years. A substantial decline occurred in the rate of growth in domestic investment and in oil output.[31] Although the economic slowdown was also associated with factors such as rising wage rates relative to labor productivity, declining excess capacity in most sectors and the appreciating ruble, the Yukos crisis exacerbated the business-government climate and badly hurt the performance of the Russian economy.

Attempting to reduce uncertainty, on November 16, 2004, President Putin affirmed:

> The state must guarantee the stability of the results of privatization and provide all possible protection for private property as one of the foundations of market economics. The state must protect private property no less than state property.[32]

As for the Yukos crisis, the president indicated that no further large-scale investigations were intended. Instructing the state bureaucrats, he pleaded that the investigation of business cases – including tax cases – should not be taken as a cue to seek threats to state interests in every newly established company. "Fear," he warned, "is unproductive."[33] Further, in his State of the Nation address to Parliament on March 25, 2005, he said, "The state bureaucracy was an isolated and sometimes an arrogant caste."[34]

The need for such presidential admonition highlights a key element in the Yukos crisis. Procedures of the prosecutor-general's office and of the Tax Ministry have damaged Russia as a destination for large-scale foreign investment in the non-energy sectors. Whatever the wrongs committed by Mikhail Khodorkovsky[35] and Yukos, the transfer of Yukos' assets, first to Baikal and then to Rosneft, did not serve as an acceptable corrective. The Yugansk auction was not free, fair, open or corrective. Private investors the world over suffered massive losses, though their decisions had been made in good faith and were based on the pronouncements of Russian authorities. The evidence indicates an urgent need to improve Russia's prosecutorial practices – even more than its laws – since long-term political stability, diversified domestic and foreign investment and robust economic growth appear to be critically at stake.[36]

Among the lessons from the Yukos crisis, it appears possible to identify the following in more general terms:

- Although responsible macroeconomic policies may be indispensable for generating long-term, robust GDP growth rates, the effectiveness of such policies may be shattered by irresponsible prosecutorial enforcement procedures. It is the combination of responsible macroeconomic policies and, more broadly, civil and effective institutional conditions that are essential for achieving and sustaining long-term high and steady economic growth rates.
- Associations between members of the business community, between professionals in health, the law and sports, teachers and the media are an essential democratic instrument for constraining the periodic zealous and authoritarian acts of official bureaucracies.

- Favorable exogenous conditions, such as extraordinarily high world prices of oil and gas, are unlikely to prevent the deceleration of robust GDP growth rates. But the responsible macroeconomic policies can play a significant role in rapidly restoring economic balance.
- Disclosure of information by public and private bodies – such as the nature of decisions regarding the magnitude of taxation and corporate bribery – is at the core of mitigating both public and private corruption.
- The coalescence of high government officials and business executives, be it in the dual role of ministers serving as executives in government-controlled companies or in collusions between government agents and private enterprise, can lead to commercial setbacks that may generate into national economic crises.
- In a globalized economy, it is both extremely difficult and politically costly for national leaders to convey a sense of balance and proportion in regard to other countries' crises. That the Yukos crisis damaged Russia's economic performance is incontrovertible, but its external economic evaluation was exaggerated. By placing major emphasis on political and economic stability, President Putin was able to constrain the crisis into a singular event rather than a multiple, indefinite phenomenon. Nevertheless, a crisis engendered domestically by destructive political and economic forces may in the long term be more costly to a nation's foreign trade and investment restructuring than to the short- and medium-term deceleration of its GDP growth rate.

6 Transitional tensions and permanent interests

A serious deterioration in relations between many Western nations and Russia has recently been recorded in the public media and by the respective governments. Grievances have been proclaimed on both sides. Russia regards the Jackson–Vanek Amendment, enacted by the Congress in 1976, as a relic of the Cold War. Legally, it ties U.S. trade benefits to Russia's emigration policy – a consideration that is no longer relevant. Clearly, the abolition of this legislation is long overdue. Although average tariff rates of the Unites States and the EU are now not high by any standards, certain sectors such as temperate-zone agricultural products, steel and light manufactures – sectors in which Russia is expected to be developing competitive advantages – are classified by the EU as "vulnerable" or "sensitive." This represents a substantial potential barrier to the expansion of Russia's exports. Similar obstacles exist in some U.S. import sectors.[1] The spring 2004 enlargement of the EU and NATO was supported by Russia on the condition that the EU would delay the imposition of higher import tariffs on "sensitive" Russian goods and remove restrictions on energy imports. Russia also asked the EU to accept higher quotas on Russian grain imports and to ease market access for Russian steel products. Unless such concessions were made, Russian officials argued, their enterprises would suffer from increased tariff barriers in the new EU member states of Central and Eastern Europe; for under present EU–Russian treaties, the latter would be allowed to export to Russia at lower tariff levels, while Russia would face higher tariff levels on some exports to them. The EU has maintained that some tariffs on Russian goods might be higher, but the average level of tariffs would be lower.[2]

Western countries, however, have expressed concern over Russia's more assertive policies in recent years both in the former Soviet countries and in what Russia regards as its historic spheres of influence. On September 20, 2003, for example, Russia launched a drive to establish an economic union called the United Economic Space (UES). The objectives were to eliminate, in the longer term, trade barriers and customs between Russia, Ukraine, Kazakhstan and Belarus. The proffered UES treaty also called for the coordination of many aspects of economic policy. Provisionally, it was to be implemented in stages, but participation in each stage would be optional. Ukraine and Belarus added so many qualifications and particular conditions to the treaty that its implementation even then appeared to be problematic.[3] In May 2003, as a result of a dispute with Belarus over its failure to accept new payment terms for gas, Russia temporarily suspended deliveries via a pipeline that also flows to other European countries – an act that generated an alarm in Poland.[4]

Much more significant are the conflicts of interest that have arisen between the United States and Russia with respect to influence in the Caucasus, Central Asia and the Middle East over the control of oil and gas reserves. Additionally, Russia faces growing pressure from the United States to remove its military forces from Georgia, particularly as the United States regards Georgia a "strategic partner" in a region considered to be a crossroad for terrorists. With the encouragement of the U.S. government and new leaders in governments bordering the Caspian Sea and in Georgia, Western countries – assisted by the International Financial Corporation of the World Bank and the EBRD – have made huge investments in some of these former Soviet republics. The states bordering on the Caspian, including Kazakhstan, Turkmenistan, Iran, Azerbaijan and Russia, are engaged in a dispute over sharing the sea's resources. Western oil companies have been cooperating with Socar, the Azerbaijan oil company, to build a pipeline extending 1,760km from Baku in Azerbaijan through Tbilisi in Georgia to the Turkish port of Ceyhan on the Mediterranean – referred to as BTC. The project has been backed by the U.S. government, and the building of the BTC line has been led by a British Petroleum 11-member consortium. Commissioners of the consortium celebrated BTC's opening on May 25, 2005, and stated that in the first few years of operation it will carry about 400,000 barrels of oil a day. Its maximum capacity is estimated at one million barrels of oil a day – slightly more than 1 percent of current global demand. BTC was specifically designed to thwart terrorist attacks; the conduit is completely buried along the path through Azerbaijan, Georgia and Turkey. Furthermore, the U.S. military has been training and equipping local security forces. Perspectives on the geopolitical effects of BTC, of course, differ: The U.S. government regards it as another alternative source of Middle East oil and gas, as well as a stabilizing factor in the region, while the Russian government has expressed concern over the increasing influence of the United States in former republics of the Soviet Union.[5] Understandably, when primarily economic issues regarding the exploration and piping of oil and gas have been fused with primarily national-security issues such

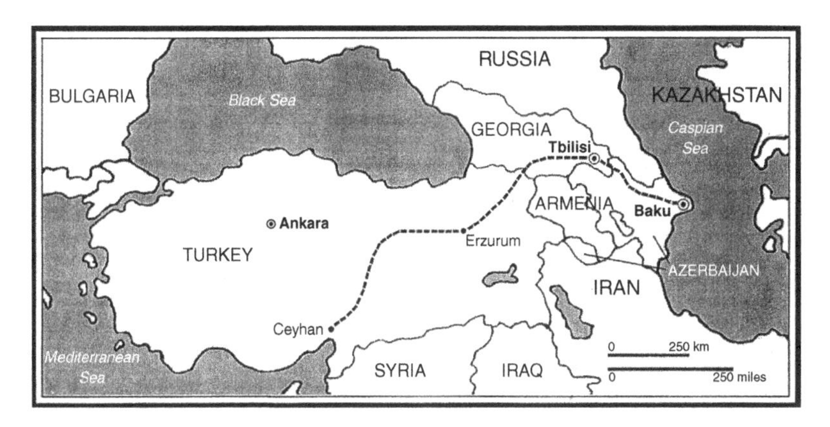

Figure 6.1 BTC (Baku–Tbilisi–Ceyhan) pipeline.

as Russia's removal of military bases from Georgia, the potential for further tensions in U.S.–Russian relations has been intensified.[6]

Thus, in February 2004, the U.S. Secretary of Defense gave Kazakhstan a security pledge in the Caspian Sea and, shortly thereafter, called on Russia to honor the tenets of its 1999 commitment to accelerate the removal of its troops from Georgia. In January 2004, the U.S. Secretary of State had comprehensive discussions with President Putin and Russian government officials, ranging from their joint interest in foreign trade, cooperation in space, counterterrorism and the spread of weapons of mass destruction. But the event was marked by an unprecedented action: the U.S. Secretary of State not only made reference to the Georgia situation and the Yukos affair but also published an essay in Izvestia appraising Russia's domestic condition. He wrote:

> Russia had yet to achieve an essential balance between the executive and other branches of government. Political power is not yet fully tethered to law.... Key aspects of civil society – free media and political party development, for example – have not yet sustained an independent presence.[7]

As a consequence of two other events, U.S.–Russian relations have deteriorated further: (1) In mid-winter 2005, as already noted, Russia briefly cut off the flow of gas to Ukraine; (2) On March 19, 2006, in a rigged election, Aleksandr G. Lukashenko was re-elected president of Belarus – an outcome condemned by all Western nations but supported by Russia.

Economic analysis and the history of international commercial policy point to the following observations in regard to tensions and conflicts between many Western countries and Russia.

Concepts

1 For economic, environmental and security reasons, the Russian government has decided that every new oil pipeline in Russia will henceforth be built and controlled by the state. "There will be no private pipelines," Russia's prime minister said, adding that, "access to the national network should be unrestricted and fair."[8] Government ownership of pipelines notwithstanding, the free and competitive access of independent producers to the pipelines for the transport of oil and gas is an indispensable condition for alleviating domestic and international conflicts. Generally, the global gains from trade are greater when the bulk of commerce is conducted by independent decision-making companies – private or official but self-governing – operating strictly on economic grounds. This tends to reduce the intrusion of national power and prestige drives into strictly commercial transactions.

2 A notable phenomenon in the EU over the last half-century has been the powerful effect of opportunity cost in mitigating serious conflicts among member states. The anticipated cost of non-compliance with key rules and procedures has deterred beggar-thy-neighbor policies. In the same manner, Russia's accession to the WTO would doubtless contribute to a lessening of tension and of conflict among the increased number of members of that organization. On May 21, 2004, after six years of negotiations, Russia reached a landmark agreement with the EU, paving the way for its entry into the WTO.[9] Russia agreed to phase out by 2013 its existing system of charges on the overflight of Siberian aviation, replacing it with a cost-based, transparent and non-discriminatory system. More generally, Russia undertook to lower import tariffs on industrial goods from 18 percent to around 8 percent; on fish products to no more than 11 percent; and on agricultural products to no more than 13 percent. Russia also agreed to open its telecommunications, transport, financial services and certain other sectors to foreign competition. By 2010, it will have increased domestic gas prices to industrial consumers by more than 100 percent. While the EU dropped its charges to the export monopoly held by Gazprom, Moscow agreed that foreign operators of gas fields in Russia would have access to Gazprom's pipeline network on terms equivalent to those enjoyed by the company's domestically

owned rivals. In the diplomatic arena, Putin pledged to speed up Russia's ratification of the Kyoto Protocol, which aims to reduce global emissions of carbon dioxide and other heat-trapping gases. On October 22, 2004, the Duma overwhelmingly ratified the protocol and on November 5, the president signed it into law. As Pascal Lamy, EU Trade Commissioner, observed:

> The WTO anchors Russia to a rule-based system, transparency and predictability, which are key for attracting foreign investment and a stimulus to a more diversified growth. This is good for Russia, good for us and good for the international trading system.[10]

In recent years, the international trading system has been affected by key Asian economies. Indeed, the East Asian Community (EAC), comprising the ten ASEAN states, China, Japan and South Korea, has been heralded as the vehicle of a "new Asian century."[11] The center of gravity with respect to Asian trade and investment has been rapidly shifting from the United States to China. Owing to the world's excess demand for energy reserves, most EAC states have an inordinate need for Russia's hydrocarbon resources. China had granted Rosneft a $6 billion loan to acquire Yugansk as a prepayment for future oil deliveries. China has also granted St. Petersburg a $1.3-billion loan to help renovate its infrastructure. Japan has agreed to provide a $5-billion loan to the Russian monopoly Transneft, which will build a pipeline from eastern Siberia to the Pacific, enabling Russia to export oil and liquefied natural gas (LNG) to Japan, to other EAC states and to the U.S. west coast.[12] Furthermore, the TNK-BP $18.5 billion joint project places much emphasis on the eastern Siberian–Pacific region. The company has launched a gradual consolidation of all its Russian subsidiaries. This reorganization is proceeding by close cooperation between the Russian government and the company, as well as the company and its minority shareholders. TNK-BP is expected to replace Yukos as Russia's largest and most efficient oil giant. The Royal Dutch Shell group has concluded an agreement with Gazprom whereby it will obtain access to Russia's largest gas development fields. The financial terms of this agreement will enable Gazprom, in turn, to acquire a stake in Exxon Mobil's Sakhalin 2 venture off Russia's Pacific coast.[13]

While the integration with the European-Atlantic Community now looms large among Russia's foreign policy objectives, its recent expansion of trade and investment with key Asian economies clearly points to the importance of increasing its integration with the AEC. At the same time, the global distribution of Russia's foreign trade and its preparation to enter the WTO suggest that conducting international economic policies predominantly on the basis of multilateral equality of treatment would elicit the most favorable responses from Russia's trading partners and yield the greatest economic returns.

4 Recent economic research has confirmed the view of economic historians that, in the long term, key institutional and structural reforms in developing and transition economies would tend to improve their economic performance.[14] A repressive regime, these studies show, is unlikely to provide a framework conducive to the achievement of both high economic growth and democratic goals. Historically, the existence of a market system and free communication media has been necessary for the exposure of entrenched monopolistic and corrupt practices. Given the extreme degree of economic concentration and monopoly power in Russian industry, a necessary condition for effective reform is the establishment of a free press and free television networks that can assist strengthened government agencies in their anti-monopoly and anti-trust activities.[15]

5 President Putin streamlined the parliamentary cabinet for his second term in office allegedly in order to reinforce the influence of liberal economic reforms by helping to speed the making and implementing of new policies. He reduced the number of members in the cabinet from 30 to 17, and the number of deputy prime ministers from six to one. He also called for greater parliamentary participation in the operation of the new administration.[16] The framework of these measures has been seriously weakened, however, by two events. First, following the Beslan terrorist attacks on September 13, 2004, President Putin proposed, and shortly thereafter the Duma enacted, legislation disallowing the election by popular vote of governors or leaders of the country's 89 regions. Henceforth, they would be chosen by local legislatures from among the president's nominees. Members of the Duma will be elected entirely on national-party lines, eliminating district races, which have hitherto elected half of the Duma's membership. Understandably, there has been widespread opposition to this restructuring, summed up in twinned essays by former president Yeltsin and former president Gorbachev.[17] Second, President Putin, fearing the loss of Moscow's influence in the "near-abroad" – particularly in Ukraine, which has historically been Russia's cultural and economic partner – campaigned overtly for Viktor F. Yanukovich, the incumbent prime minister, before the presidential election of November 21, 2004. Upon the Central Election Commission's announcement

of Yanukovich as the winner, President Putin congratulated him, and the Russian Parliament unanimously recognized Yanukovich as the president-elect. But the losing candidate, Viktor A. Yushchenko – who had served as head of Ukraine's Central Bank, who was prime minister from 1999 to 2001 and who was viewed as pro-Western – declared that he had been denied his rightful victory, accusing the authoritarian administration of corruption and massive electoral fraud. European and American monitors of the election confirmed the truth of these allegations. Both the Ukraine Supreme Court and the Parliament passed non-binding pronouncements excoriating the vote. Mass protests clogged the center of Kiev, paralyzing the government, roiling the economy and raising the specter of civil conflict. In a milestone decision, on December 3, 2004, the Ukraine Supreme Court pronounced that the Central Election Commission was guilty of unlawful conduct, rendering a clear determination of the winner impossible. The court declared the election invalid and ordered a rerun between the candidates by December 26. Meanwhile, President Leonid D. Kuchma, who had held meetings on the crisis with the two candidates, with European statesmen and with President Putin, announced on December 8 that the Parliament had reached fundamental compromises to reform the law for the purpose of minimizing electoral fraud and to amend the constitution for the purpose of shifting certain powers from the authoritarian presidency to the Parliament. These reforms constituted a significant advance toward a central European model of parliamentary democracy. In the long term, they may serve the national interests of Ukraine, Russia and Western nations. However, the events that precipitated the reforms had the immediate effect of exacerbating the tensions and divisions not only between east and west Ukraine, but palpably between Russia and the West. On December 26, 2004, a rerun of the election was held and Viktor A. Yushchenko won with 51.9 percent of the vote, as against 44.4 percent for his rival.[18]

6 Regarding the controversial issue of how the Russian prosecutor-general's office pursues fraud, tax evasion and corruption charges, economic "agency theory" suggests a way forward. It would recognize a dual role for cabinet members: first, to serve as monitors controlling government bureaucracy; second, to represent the president. If the designated functions were not performed, they would face dismissal from office.[19] Within this framework, a cabinet minister could be appointed to monitor lobbying of members of the Duma and to provide oversight on law enforcement.

7 In Western countries, and particularly in former Soviet states, the

legacy of the Soviet era has left a deep distrust of the Russian government and of its state-controlled companies, irrespective of the fact that national interest has impelled the Russian government scrupulously to meet its contractual obligations. In Russia, the legacy of history has bequeathed xenophobia of western bankers, direct investors and non-government organizations (NGOs), even when they conduct affairs according to international standards.

Implementing the new agenda

1 A significant emphasis in Russia's new agenda for the innovative restructuring of the economy centers on the view that Russian companies – be they government-controlled or privately owned – will conduct their affairs on economic, market-driven terms. This policy, if reasonably well implemented, could reduce conflicts among both governments and entrepreneurs of Russia and the West. Presently, however, Russia's first deputy prime minister serves as chairman of Gazprom, and the deputy chief of the presidential administration serves as chairman of Rosneft. Conflicts of interest between such political and corporate responsibilities are inevitable. The removal of coalescence between the high offices of government and positions of corporate leadership is, therefore, essential for the credible implementation of the market-oriented proposal, which is consistent with the theory and practice of international commercial policy.
2 Energy is at the core of Russia's restructuring program. For Putin, its foundations have a long history. In 1997, as a part-time student at the State Mining Institute, he wrote a dissertation entitled, "Mineral Raw Materials in the Strategy for Development of the Russian Economy."[20] Russia's rich natural resources, he argued, would secure not only its economic future but also its international position. He presented a scenario in which large state-controlled – but in part privately financed – industrial corporations would be able to compete with Western multinationals. According to the new agenda, fortunate historic conditions now make this feasible. The program incorporates the following:

   - Appointing Western experts to serve as directors in major Russian companies;
   - Modernizing Russia's financial structure and promoting foreign direct investment, especially in the discovery and exploration of new energy fields.
   - Ensuring Western energy security by increasing the economic

interdependence of Russian and Western companies. Russian officials emphasize the importance of negotiating agreements on the basis of reciprocity – in particular, the exchange of access to investment and production in Russian energy companies for investment and production opportunities in western European and American refining operations and retail fuel sales.[21]

- Negotiating contracts with both Western countries and former Soviet states for comparatively long periods of time, but at prices that reflect those in the world market. The aim is to eliminate, as soon as contracts expire, the huge subsidies that Russia has granted to Soviet successor nations. Putin believes this is the fairest, the most transparent and the most reliable basis for pricing policy. With some exceptions, it is to be implemented in the medium term.

3 The Russian government has already begun to appoint notable Western officials and technical experts to the boards of major Russian companies. Putin has appointed Gerhard Schroder, former chancellor of Germany, chairman of the North European Gas Pipeline Company – a 51 percent subsidiary of Gazprom. He also invited Donald Evans, former U.S. secretary of commerce, to chair Rosneft. Evans politely declined, and Putin then appointed Peter O'Brien, a Morgan Stanley vice president in Moscow, to the board of Rosneft.[22]

4 The agenda calls for modernizing Russia's financial structure and promoting foreign direct investment especially for the innovative restructuring of the energy industry. The process appears to be cumulative. Russia is the world's largest gas producer, providing one-quarter of western European natural gas imports. During the first four months of 2006, Gazprom gained $100 billion in market value to become the fourth largest publicly traded company in the world.[23] The creation of the North European Gas Pipeline Company represented a German investment of about $5 billion in Russia. The richest Russian oligarch, Roman Abramovich, now living in London, has entered negotiations to buy a 40 percent stake in Evraz, Russia's largest steel producer.[24] Rosneft is poised to issue an initial public offering (IPO) estimated at $10 billion.[25]

5 Global conditions of energy demand and supply are consistent with Russia's program.[26] On the demand side, world crude oil consumption rose 2 percent in 2003 and surged to 4 percent in 2004 – the largest yearly increase in a quarter century.[27] However, in 2005, the rise in the price of oil decelerated the global rate of consumption to 1.3 percent. Nonetheless, the absolute level of oil consumption was

extremely high relative to earlier expectations. Moreover, at the end of the first half of 2006, strong oil demand pressures had resumed, with forward market prices for oil rising in tandem with spot market prices.

On the supply side, the production of oil has been constrained by factors such as availability, terrorism, weather-related disasters and geopolitics. Spare capacity in the Organization of Petroleum Exporting Countries (OPEC) has recently been eliminated. In some of these countries, incentives to expand output have been counterbalanced by the possibility of lower prices in the future. Political turmoil in Iraq, Iran, Nigeria and Venezuela has further reduced the growth rate in supply. Consequently, despite high world prices for oil in 2005, the rate of growth in oil production flattened. Global supply conditions were compounded by two recent hurricanes in the United States, Katrina and Rita, which reduced U.S. production by nearly 2 percent of world output. In toto, therefore, futures markets indicate that the probability of oil prices dropping back to 1990 levels is extremely remote.

The situation with respect to gas is not dissimilar. On the demand side, as the price of oil soared, substitution effects for natural gas increased; especially as LNG is a clean-burning fuel. Demand for LNG has also been rising because the demand for sweet, light fuels is mismatched to the supply of heavy, sulfurous ones. On the supply side, geological and transit constraints on gas have been no less pronounced than those on crude oil. Thus, in the 1990s, the price of LNG in the U.S. averaged $2 per 1,000 cubic meters Btu. In 2005, the price was $9, and it peaked at $15 following the hurricanes. Futures markets estimate the price for LNG in the medium term at $9 per 1,000 cubic meters Btu.

Prevailing expectations, therefore, are consistent with Russia's program, placing major emphasis on expanding energy production. However, while western European countries are heavily dependent on Russian oil and gas, they have recently expressed concern over Russia's reliability and security as a supplier.

The Russia–Ukraine conflict over the price and shutdown of gas exacerbated accumulating tensions between Russia and the West. After a year's unsuccessful negotiations between Russian officials and those of Ukraine, on December 30, 2005, the executive head of Gazprom notified the Ukraine government — doubtless with Putin's approval – that if Ukraine did not accept the world price for natural gas, the company would suspend shipment to Ukraine.[28] The subsidized price that Ukraine had been paying for natural gas was $50 per

1,000 cubic meters Btu. The price Russia was charging western European countries was between $220 and $230 per 1,000 cubic meters Btu. Viktor A. Yushchenko, President of Ukraine, declined Gazprom's suggested terms, proposing that the price be frozen at $50 and the supply of gas maintained until January 10, 2006, pending further negotiations. The next day, December 31, Putin instructed Gazprom to keep selling gas to Ukraine at the $50 price until the end of March 2006, on the condition that Ukraine would agree to pay market prices for gas beginning April 1, 2006. Putin also offered Ukraine a loan of $3.6 billion to cover the additional costs. Yushchenko replied that Ukraine could pay its own extra costs. Furthermore, the prime minister of Ukraine notified Gazprom that his government would agree to a gradual transition to world market prices, but at a more gradual pace than proposed by Moscow, with details to be negotiated. He also cautioned that, since gas shipped to other European countries passed through the same pipeline, in the event of emergency, Ukraine might have to draw on those supplies. The executive head of Gazprom exclaimed: "That would be theft!"[29] Putin found the pronouncements of the Ukraine government unacceptable. He gave them until midnight on December 31 to accept his terms. Ukraine officials played down the probability that Russia would resort to a shutdown of gas supplies or an immediate large price increase. The EU suggested a meeting of Russian, Ukrainian and European energy officials on January 4, 2006. Gazprom reiterated the threat: "If Ukraine does not sign a contract on the purchase of gas in the remaining hours before the start of the New Year, on January 1, at 10 a.m., Moscow time, gas supplies from the territory of the Russia Federation to Ukraine will be completely cut off."[30] On Sunday, January 1, 2006, at the stated time, Gazprom reduced the flow of gas into the pipeline by 20 percent. Ukraine removed 90 million cubic meters of gas that was being shipped to other European countries. Heavy criticism and pressure were directed at Russia by the International Energy Agency (IEA), by the EU and by the governments of Germany, France, Italy and the United States. By the end of Tuesday, January 2, Gazprom had restored normal supplies. On January 4, 2006, Russia and Ukraine signed a five-year face-saving agreement. Russia would be paid the world market price of $230 per 1,000 cubic meters Btu, but by mixing Russian supplies with gas from Turkmenistan and Kazakhstan, the net bundled price to Ukraine would be $95.

6 The entire affair has highlighted the importance of establishing a mechanism to deal with such potential controversies. The European

Energy Charter was designed, in effect, to secure greater reliability, as well as freer trade and investment, in the field of energy. Most European countries have signed and ratified the charter. Russia has signed but ratification awaits agreement on incorporating principles of reciprocity into the document.[31] Britain and Germany have expressed agreement with these principles. The ratification and implementation of a revised charter could not only prevent the sort of costly discord that was associated with the Russia–Ukraine crisis, but could help build the foundation – under law – for greater international energy security.

7 The financial structure of large Russian companies is being multinationalized. Russia is the world's biggest exporter of natural gas and second biggest exporter of crude oil. Gazprom, Russia's largest company, is the world's largest gas producer; it provides about one-quarter of west European gas imports. In the first four months of 2006, Gazprom gained $100 billion in market value to become the fourth-largest publicly traded company in the world.[32] Attention has already been drawn to the TNK-BP huge merger. The establishment of the North European Gas Pipeline Company embodied a German investment of $5 billion. The richest Russian oligarch, now living in London, has entered negotiations to buy a 40-percent stake in Evraz, Russia's largest steel producer.[33] Rosneft is poised to issue an IPO on London's stock exchange at an estimated $10–$11 billion.[34]

These signs of financial confidence in the Russian economy, coupled with an enlarged inflow of direct foreign investment, have been greatly influenced by long-term expectations on the role of Russia as a supplier of energy for the world economy.

8 Regarding the consolidation of Russia's industries, the agenda concentrates on the formation of mergers for the express purpose of increasing productivity and profitability. From 2000 to 2005, the proportion of loss-making companies in Russia was declining but extremely high. The figure in 2005 was still 33.5 percent. Moreover, the real average wage rate in industry was above the index in productivity, contributing to a loss of industrial competitiveness. An improvement appears to have occurred in 2005 (Appendices II.1–II.2). However, a recent report on Russia's foreign trade for 2005 indicates that the country's intra-industry trade has been very low and declining steadily.[35] Generally, exports of manufactured goods had been unable to maintain global competitiveness. The increasing integration of the Russian economy into the world economy has therefore been dependent on its inter-industry specialization, on the export of natural-resource products and imports of high-technology products. Also, during the first half of 2006, Russia's real effective exchange rate, which has been

rising, appreciated another 4 percent, further reducing competitiveness of non-energy products. On July 1, 2006, Russia adopted "full" convertibility of the ruble.[36] While consistent with the new economic agenda, it is likely to reduce further Russia's competitiveness in manufactured goods.

Understandably, the program to consolidate industry has strong support in the Duma. Mergers are expected to occur among small- and medium-sized companies as well as among such giant corporations as in the aviation and automotive industries. An illustrative event has already occurred. On February 21, 2006, President Putin signed a decree creating a huge aviation entity, combining the nation's six major aircraft manufacturing and design companies into a single holding corporation. Under the decree, Russia will focus on producing smaller regional passenger jets and on military and transport aircraft. An industry that was de facto bankrupt will be able to specialize in fields where Russia appears to have a comparative advantage. "This is a real important change," one analyst has said. "The merger puts design bureaus and production assets under one roof."[37] Aviation experts in Moscow believe that, with shared engineering and manufacturing skills, the new company could make Russian manufacturing a formidable competitor in Western markets. The strategy, in fact, is one of partnership with assistance from aviation giants such as Boeing and Airbus. Boeing, in fact, serves as advisor to the new entity, called United Aircraft Corporation.

In the automotive sector, where many companies were badly managed, even limited consolidation has led to substantial rises in productivity. Integration into large industrial conglomerates has provided access to the much needed capital. In the case of Gazprom and the German chemicals company BASF, an asset swap was used to arrange a joint venture for the sale of Russian natural gas in Europe in exchange for BASF's participation in a gas field in western Siberia. In implementing the agenda, the government is establishing special economic zones, and assisting small- and medium-size firms – technically and financially – with the objective of expanding high-tech production for the domestic and export markets.

Positive as these measures may be, recent research and experience in Western countries have shown that plans for industrial consolidation often provide the kind of intellectual light that blinds rather than guides. An important lesson may be cogent for the Russian agenda. Many firms that are de facto bankrupt should be compelled, by market forces, to exit.[38] This is particularly relevant to many small, undercapitalized and inefficient banks.

9 Investing in people is designated a significant role in the agenda. In 2005, the Russian Parliament moderately increased the allocation of funds to help implement national priorities in education, health care, affordable housing and agriculture. These are all long-term investments. They are related to the attempt of overcoming the crisis in demography; Russia has been losing 700,000 people per year. President Putin has launched a ten-year program with particular emphasis on providing subsidies to increase the birth rate.

The Russian government has been implementing fiscal policy in a commendable way. Nonetheless, three controversial issues deserve attention.

- First, several members of the Duma have strongly suggested that the Fiscal Stabilization Fund be used to expand current social expenditures. Fundamentally, the fund is an oil stabilization fund. It has been growing rapidly; as of July 1, 2006, the windfall gains of crude oil amounted to $70 billion. It would be ill-advised to utilize the fund for current social expenditures. Experience of other countries has indicated that stabilization funds could readily be misused. Maintaining long-term fiscal balance and contributing to long-term economic development and growth appear to be efficacious objectives of an oil stabilization fund.
- Second, the establishment of "full" convertibility of the ruble has been an aim of the agenda and could be a powerful mechanism in the regulation of the economy. Experience with financial crises in transition economies strongly suggests, however, that it should be managed to prevent rapid increases, or decreases, in the real effective value of the exchange rate. As a quasi-market economy, Russia can use interest-rate mechanisms and administrative controls to decelerate the rate of inflation and to prevent volatile fluctuations of the ruble.
- Third, concerns have been expressed over the danger of Dutch disease in Russia. One distinguished authority has rightly maintained that this likelihood may be negligible. The proportion of energy in Russia's GDP is estimated at 15–25 percent. This constitutes a lower proportion than in most OPEC countries. In recent years, the Russian government has managed its macroeconomic policies in an exemplary way. The Fiscal Stabilization Fund could contribute to the maintenance of economic stability. In addition, accelerating banking reform would assist the regulation of both monitoring and exchange rate policies. Under such conditions, Russia may well be able to prevent Dutch disease.[39]

If the analysis of this study is reasonably correct, Western countries have a long-term and permanent interest in the health of the Russian economy. In effect, without the cooperation of Russia, Western countries cannot effectively act on the most critical issues of the global war on terrorism, of resolving the problems with Iraq, Iran, North Korea, the Middle East and the Caucusus – as well as those of global warming and international energy security. An expansion of responsible economic interdependence between the European-Atlantic Community and Russia – under a strengthened energy charter – would both reduce international tensions and make the implementation of Russia's economic agenda more secure.

7 Concluding observations

Russia is breaking out from historic cataclysms into the global economy. The material and analysis presented in this study suggest that the long-term success of the transition will be contingent on the following conditions.

- Recent research in economic history has shown that modern economic growth may be achieved in ways other than those marked by the British industrial revolution.[1] Such growth can occur without a highly concentrated industrial breakthrough. If a country is in possession of an educated population, a rich agricultural base and an ample energy sector, it can obtain broadly diversified economic development with high and sustainable growth rates. Russia, it has been shown, largely fulfills these conditions. In an enabling politico-economic environment, it would therefore be able to utilize its natural resource sectors as engines of transition toward specialization in high-valued manufactures and in high-tech industries. Moreover, in these fields, Russia is in a position to focus on both high-wage and low-wage markets. This form of diversified transformation constitutes the critical challenge facing Russia.
- Presently, Russia has insufficient human physical capital to modernize its energy industries or to build the necessary infrastructures for its nascent high-tech industries. Attaining these objectives will require greatly increased foreign direct investment in shared projects. Historically, however, Russia has suffered from xenophobia in regard to foreign investment. This was often a reaction to egregious exploitation by a small number of foreign countries and a few monopolistic trading companies. These conditions no longer prevail. Although comparatively small, foreign investment in Russia is now multifarious and global. The danger of a small number of foreigners misusing their ownership of a large volume of shares in Russian companies has been substantially reduced. But the xenophobia remains, especially among

older officials in the central and regional governments, as well as in the older population at large. Russia is in need of a government-sponsored educational program – comprehensive and reiterative – to promote a hospitable environment for foreign investment. This would greatly contribute to achieving President Putin's twin goals of diversifying the Russian economy and doubling its GDP by 2012.

- Even though Russia's GDP growth rate in 2003 and 2004 was above 7 percent, the evidence indicates that the Yukos crisis materially damaged the performance of the economy. Not surprisingly, the crisis also had an effect on the relationship between business and government. The oligarchs no longer act as independent agents confronting the government. In general, the relationship between business and government has become more cooperative. But prosecutorial excess has tarnished Russia's image abroad. Consequently, foreign investment in the non-energy sectors has remained in the order of "second smalls." With the Yukos crisis coming to an end, the Russian government has the opportunity to take concrete and consistent steps to improve legal procedures and the rule of law, to advance economic reforms and to invigorate the battle against crime and corruption. There should be a standard forum between Russian economists and those of Western countries and Asia to break down old barriers and to coordinate approaches to foreign investment, regulation and competition. A "demonstration project" between Russian and foreign investors should also be developed to demonstrate internationally what could be accomplished by cooperative economic development, as can be seen embryonically in the TNK-BP venture. Such actions would reduce the frictions between Russia and foreign governments as well as those between Russian and foreign entrepreneurs.
- Transforming Russian agriculture is a core economic problem for Russia. In virtually all developed nations, an agricultural revolution has substantially reduced the proportion of the labor force in agriculture and has been a prerequisite for successful economic advance – an event which has yet to occur in Russia. While the conditions for a major transformation of Russia's agriculture are many and complex, a fundamental systemic effort in this sector is overdue. Heavy investment in R&D and organized agricultural research are called for. There is cumulative evidence in the United States and other countries that geneticists and botanists have markedly improved the productivity of many crops. Extension services have fostered advances in agricultural technology. Government and, most recently, commercial enterprises have produced the means of higher yields in many products. A focused program sponsored by Russia's federal and regional governments to

raise factor productivity in agriculture will be necessary to raise the GDP growth rate and to mitigate the inequality of income distribution between rural and urban areas.

- As noted, Russia's long-term success in economic development is contingent on establishing a satisfactory environment for a high and sustained level of private investment. However, in the recent transition, Russia's economic and political progress has been seriously hampered by a trilemma: a quasi-market system, a destructive bureaucracy and systemic corruption. These conditions had the effect not only of decelerating the rate of growth in domestic and foreign investment, but also of impeding Russia's advance into the global economy. The erratic and arbitrary prosecutorial procedures disrupted the tax administration, harmed the business climate and undermined confidence in property rights and the rule of law. In analyzing the causes of these events, and attendant economic conditions, this study has drawn attention to the application of economic "agency theory," the fostering of an untrammeled media and the establishment of an independent judiciary to provide the vital instrumental means for Russia's "break out."
- The major objective of this work was to show that there is a solid, strategic foundation for the expansion of trade and investment between Western countries and Russia. Three phases have been identified in which Russia has achieved a successful economic transition. The next phase would benefit from further coordination of domestic and international economic codes. In this process – including accession into the WTO – the task of integrating Russia with the European-Atlantic Community is great and arduous, but not greater than the need.

Appendices

Appendix I

Table I.1 Russian federation: main economic indicators, 2000–2005

	2000	*2001*	*2002*	*2003*	*2004*	*2005*
Output indicators						
GDP (% of previous year)	10.0	5.1	4.7	7.3	7.2	6.4
Industrial production (% change, y-o-y)	11.9	4.9	3.7	7.0	8.3	4.0
Extraction of mineral resources (% change, y-o-y)	–	–	6.8	8.7	6.8	1.3
Fixed capital investment (% change, y-o-y)	17.4	8.7	2.6	12.5	10.9	10.5
Fiscal and monetary indicators						
Federal government balance (% GDP)	2.3	3.0	3.2	1.7	4.2	7.5
Consolidated budget balance (% GDP)	–	–	–	1.3	4.5	7.7
M2 (% change, p-o-p)	–	44.6	34.1	44.8	42.5	35.6
Inflation (CP1), (% change, p-o-p)	20.2	18.6	15.1	12.0	11.7	10.9
GDP deflator	–	16.5	15.7	14.0	19.5	19.6
Nominal exchange rate (average)	–	29.2	31.4	30.7	28.8	28.3
Real effective exchange rate July 1998=100 (IMF)	67.0	79.4	82.0	90.5	103.7	112.6
Real effective exchange rate % change, p-o-p (IMF)	–	18.7	3.3	10.3	14.5	8.7
Stabilization fund (billion $, end-o-p)	–	–	–	–	18.7	42.9
Reserves (including gold) (billion $, end-o-p)	28.0	36.6	47.8	76.9	124.5	182.2
Balance and payment indicators						
Trade balance (billion $)	60.7	48.1	46.3	59.9	86.9	118.3
Share of energy resources in export of goods (%)	–	51.2	52.4	54.2	54.7	61.1
Current account (billion $)	46.3	33.9	29.1	35.4	58.6	84.2
Export of goods (billion $)	105.6	101.9	107.3	135.9	183.2	243.6
Import of goods (billion $)	44.9	53.8	61.0	76.1	96.3	125.3
Gross FDI (mln U.S.$ 1/)	–	3,980.0	4.002.0	6,781.0	9,420.0	13,072.0

continued

Table I.1 continued

	2000	*2001*	*2002*	*2003*	*2004*	*2005*
Average export price of Russia's oil ($/bbl)	24.0	20.9	21.0	23.9	34.1	45.2
Financial market indicators						
Average weighted lending rate for enterprises (%)	24.3	17.9	15.8	13.1	11.5	10.9
CBR refinancing rate (%, end-o-p)	25.0	25.0	21.0	16.0	13.0	12.0
Net credits to real sector/GDP (%)	–	5.4	4.4	6.8	7.1	7.4
Stock market index (RTS, ruble term)	142.4	260.1	359.1	567.3	614.1	1,125.6
Enterprise finances						
Share of loss-making companies	41.6	38.4	43.4	41.3	35.8	33.5
Profitability (net profit/sales) (%)	32.7	25.6	17.4	20.7	25.5	–
Share of credits in capital investment	–	–	10.8	14.5	15.2	13.8
Non-cash settlements (% of total sales)	30.7	22.3	18.0	14.2	11.1	–
Income, poverty and labor market						
Real disposable income (99=100)	112.0	121.7	135.3	155.4	170.8	185.8
Net change in government wage arrears (% over previous period)	–51.4	–26.5	–5.2	–34.4	–55.5	–
Average dollar wage (U.S.$)	80.2	112.4	138.6	179.4	237.2	301.6
Share of people living below subsistence (%)	28.9	27.3	24.2	20.6	17.8	15.8
Unemployment (% ILO definition)	10.4	9.0	8.1	8.6	8.2	7.6

Sources: Adapted from Worldbank Database, May 2004; *Worldbank Russian Economic Report*, March 2005 and April 2006.

Appendix II

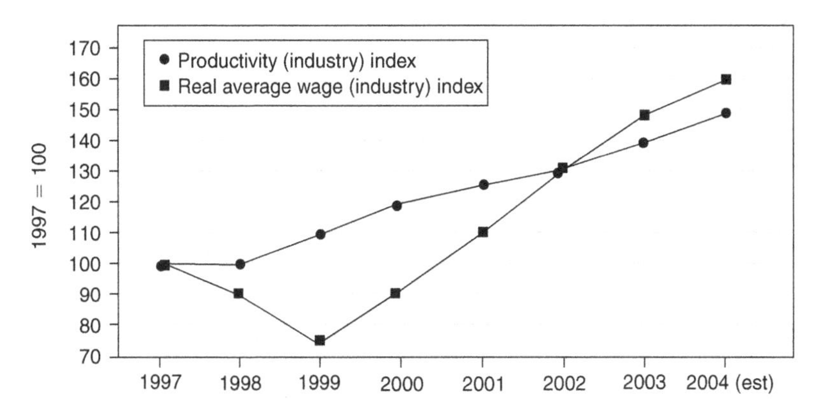

Figure II.1 Russian federation: productivity and real wage growth in industry, 1997–2004 (source: World Bank, *Russian Economic Report*, March 2005).

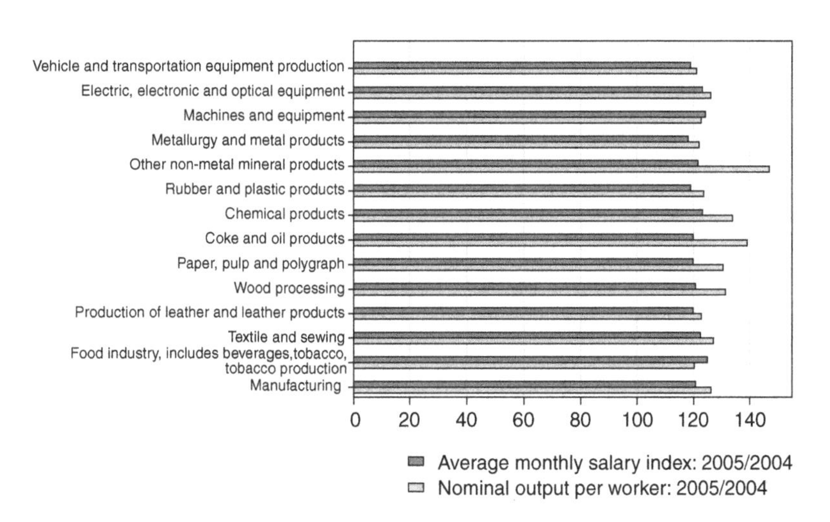

Figure II.2 Growth in output per worker and wages in industry during 2005 (current rubles) (source: Rosstat).

Appendix III

Russia's key economic indicators, 1991–1997

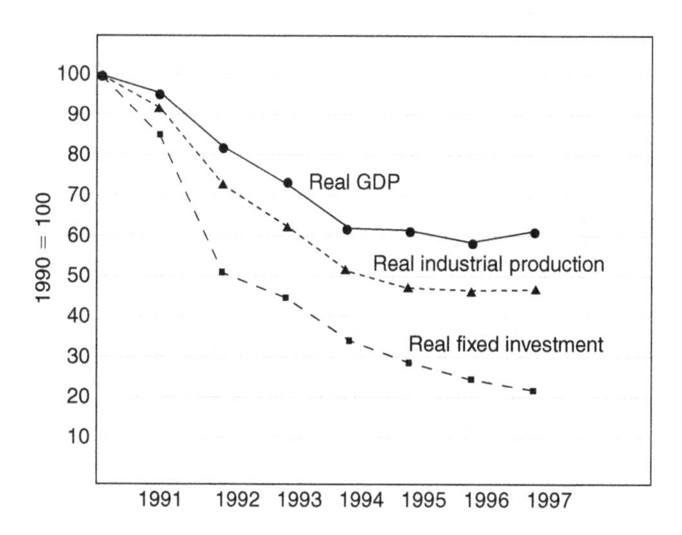

Figure III.1

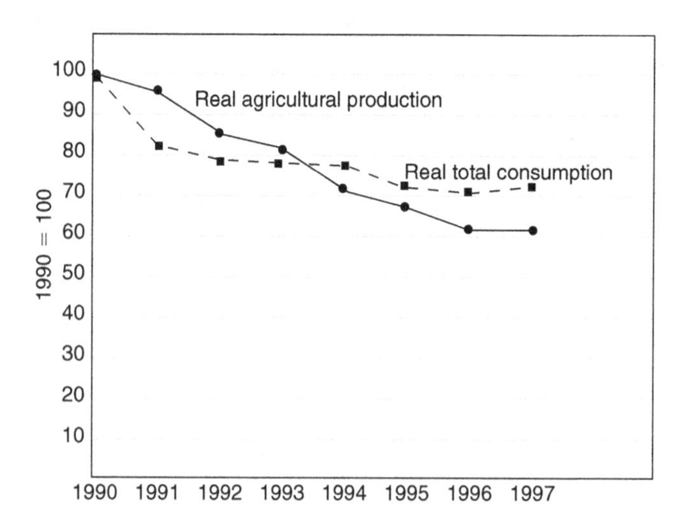

Figure III.2

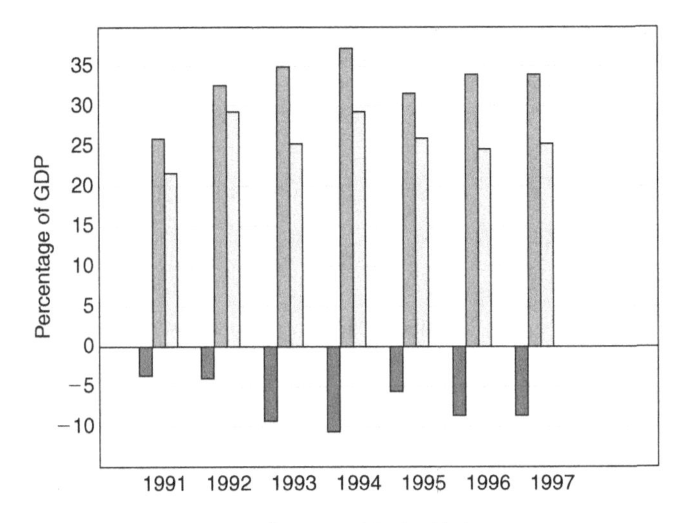

Figure III.3

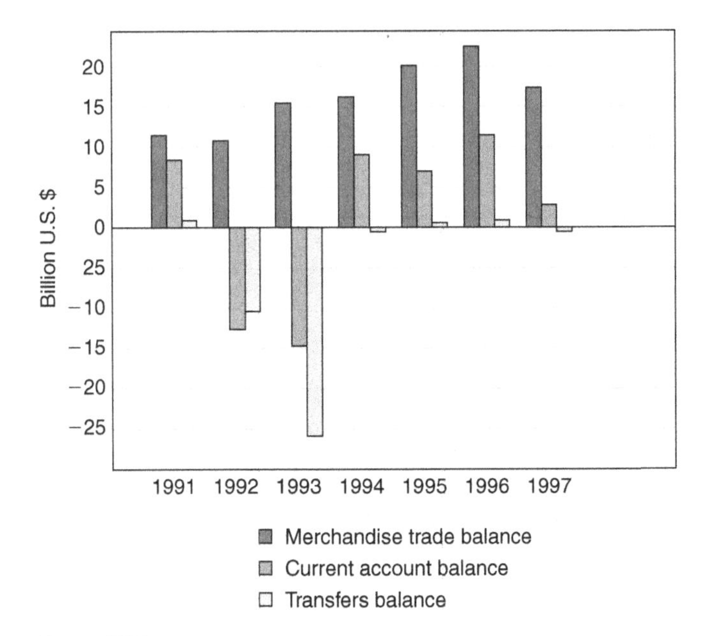

Figure III.4

Table III.1

	1991	*1992*	*1993*	*1994*	*1995*	*1996*	*1997*
M2 supply end-year (% change)	125.9	642.6	416.1	197.9	98.1	30.3	25.4
1–30 day Interbank lending rate, average	n/a	n/a	140.0	118.0	190.4	47.7	23.6
Consumer prices, Dec. to Dec. (% change)	160.3	2,508.8	844.2	214.7	131.3	21.8	11.3

Table III.2

(1990=100)	*1991*	*1992*	*1993*	*1994*	*1995*	*1996*	*1997*
Real exports of goods and services	72.0	59.8	66.6	76.0	90.4	97.7	101.4
Real imports of goods and services	54.0	44.8	46.2	55.4	66.9	65.5	68.5

Table III.3

	1991	*1992*	*1993*	*1994*	*1995*	*1996*	*1997*
Unemployment rate	n/a	2.9	5.3	7.1	8.3	9.1	9.3
Exchange rate, end-year (Rubles/U.S.$)	0.169	0.415	1.247	3.550	4.640	5.556	5.960

Sources: WEFA Group, *Eurasia Economic Outlook* (Philadelphia, Pennsylvania, Fourth Quarter 1998), pp. 3–4; and data provided by Dr. Silvana Malle, Head, Central and Eastern European Division, OECD, Paris.

Appendix IV

Russia's key economic indicators, 1998–2000

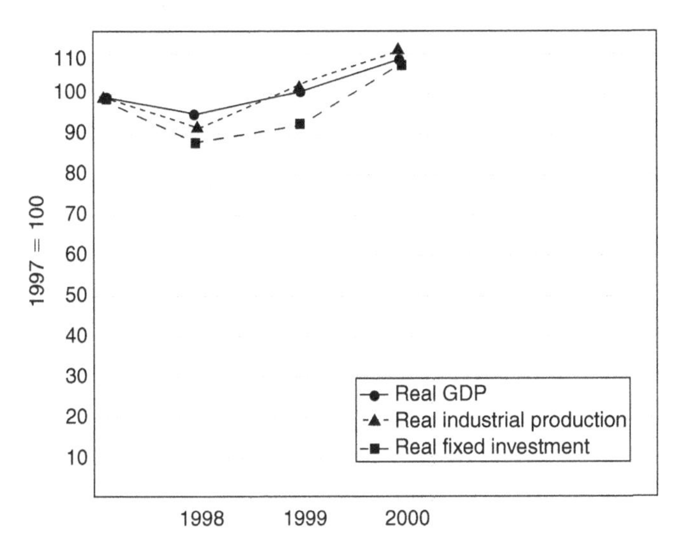

Figure IV.1

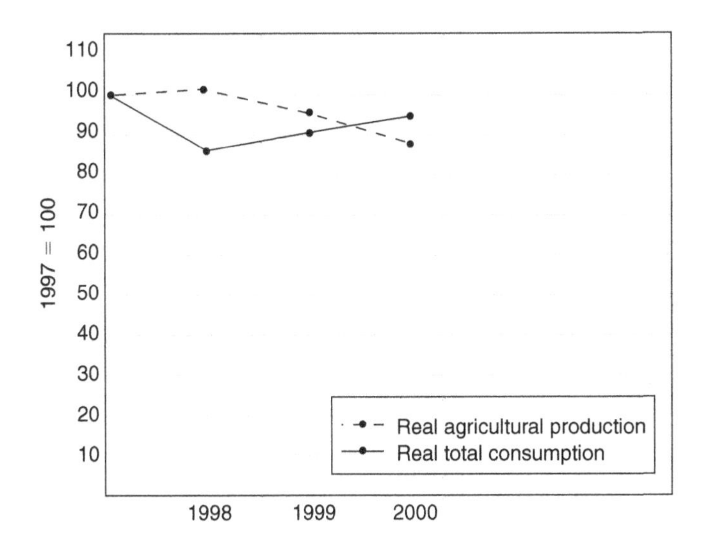

Figure IV.2

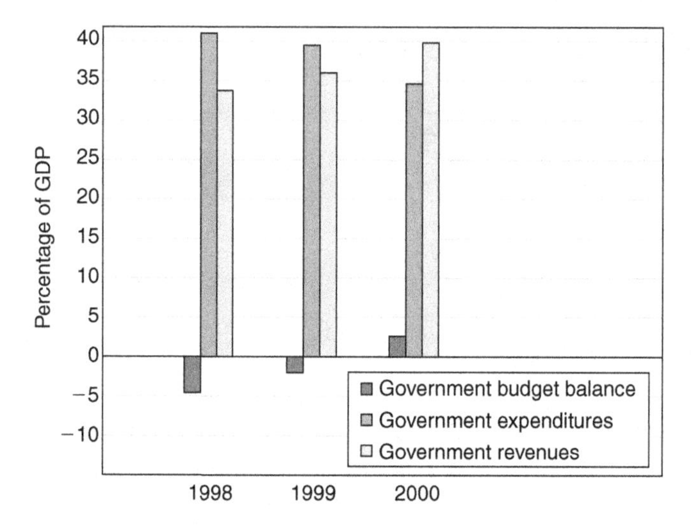

Figure IV.3

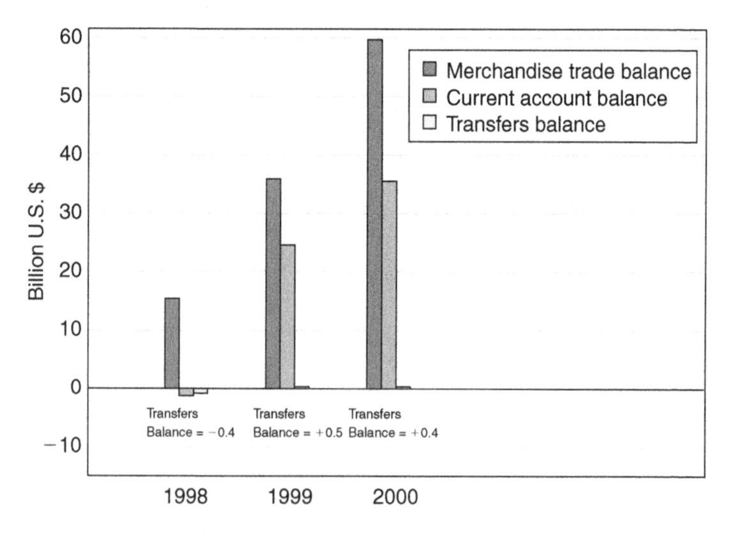

Figure IV.4

Table IV.1

	1998	*1999*	*2000*
M2 supply end-year (% change)	36.3	57.2	62.4
Consumer prices Dec. to Dec. (% change)	84.5	36.6	20.1

Table IV.2 Real effective exchange rate index (1995–2000)

(Est.)	*1995*	*1996*	*1997*	*1998*	*1999*	*2000*
Exchange rate	n/a	2.9	5.3	7.1	8.3	9.1
Exports as % of GDP	24.5	21.6	20.4	27.7	40.4	44.6
Imports as % of GDP	9.3	7.9	8.9	11.9	11.7	10.9

Note
1995–1997 average = 100.

Table IV.3

	1998	*1999*	*2000*
Unemployment rate	11.2	13.3	11.9

Table IV.4

(billion U.S.$)	*1998*	*1999*	*2000*
Gross international reserves	12.1	12.6	21.1
Net prices international reserves	–6.5	–3.0	3.6

Sources: WEFA Group, *Eurasia Economic Outlook* (Philadelphia, Pennsylvania, Fourth Quarter 1998), pp. 3–4; and data provided by Dr. Silvana Malle, Head, Central and Eastern European Division, OECD, Paris; GOSKOMSTAT, Ministry of Finance; Russian authorities.

Appendix V

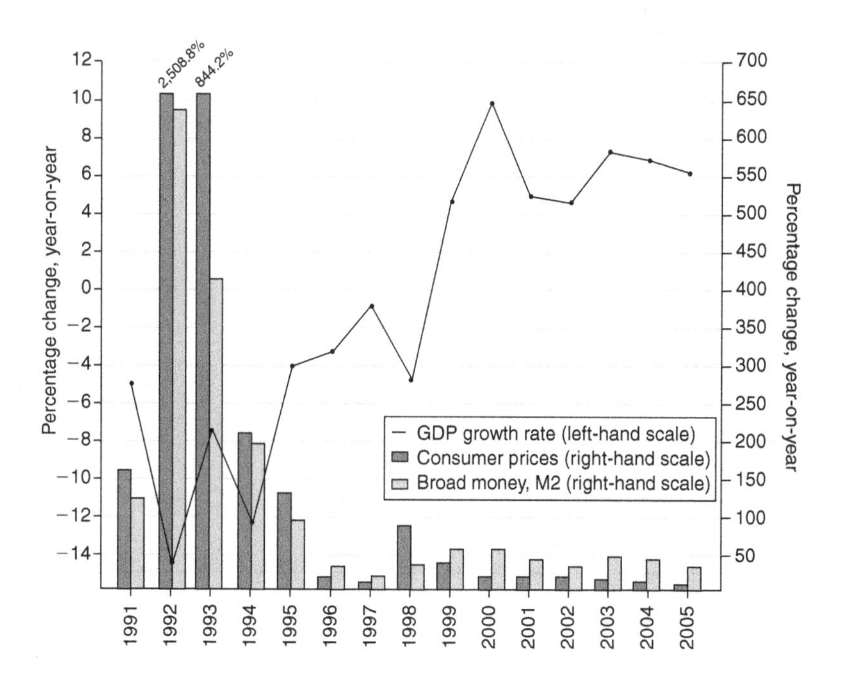

Figure V.1 Russian federation: GDP growth rate, consumer prices, and broad money (M2), 1991–2005 (sources: GDP growth rate, see Table 1 infra; Consumer prices (CPI), see Appendix III, Figure 5, and Appendix IV, Figure 5 infra; *Russian Economic Trends* (Moscow 2002), No. 3, Table 1, p. 17; M2, and RET: CBR (2002) No. 3, Appendix, Table D21, p. 117; OECD, *Economic Outlook* (Paris, June 2003/1), No. 73, Table III.2, p. 116, Goskomstat. IMF, Russian Federation, *Statistical Appendix* (September 2004), Appendix I, Infra; World Bank, *Russian Economic Report*, April 2006, Table 10, p. 24).

Appendix VI

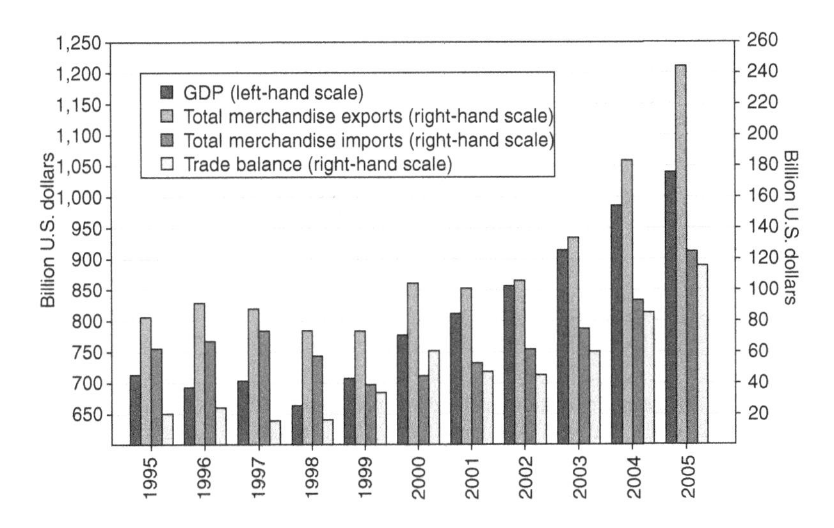

Figure VI.1 Russian federation: GDP, total merchandise exports, total merchandise imports and trade balance, 1995–2005 (sources: See Table I infra for data on GDP; European Centre for Economic Policy, Russian Economic Trends (Moscow 2002), No. 3, Appendix Table D5, p. 107 for data on merchandise exports and imports, IMF, Russian Federation, Statistical Appendix, September 2004, Table 8; Appendix I, infra; for 2005, see Appendix I).

Appendix VII

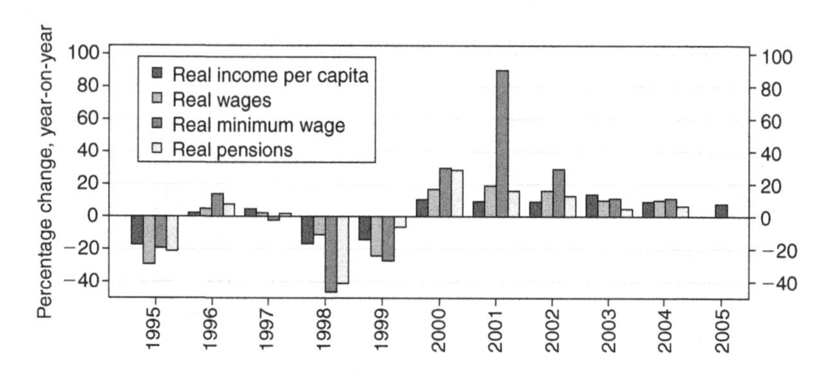

Figure VII.1 Russian federation: real income per capita, real wages, real minimum wage and real pensions, 1995–2005 (Sources: Goskomstat, IMF, *Russian Federation*, Statistical Appendix, September 2004, Table 13, p. 18; Federal State Statistics Service; Ministry of Labor; Pension Fund).

Notes

1 Russia's economic restructuring since the 1998 crisis

1 According to the OECD, it was "a common perception that the [Russian] federal government had become too weak in the 1990s even to enforce its own laws." OECD, *Russian Federation Economic Surveys, 2000–2002* (Paris: OECD, 2002), p. 168. In fact, by 1998, the disillusionment with respect to the political-economic reforms had critically reduced the credibility in the belief that the evolution of democratic governance was irreversible. This view was frequently expressed by members of the Duma, scientists and economists at an international conference of the Ioffe Physico-Technical Institute held in St. Petersburg, September 28–October 2, 1998. As the then-president Vaclav Havel of the Czech Republic had already noted, an uncertain society was being born where practically everything was possible and almost nothing was certain. *New York Times* (September 17, 1998), pp. 1A, 6A.

2 Angus Maddison, *The World Economy, A Millennial Perspective, 0–1998 A.D.* (Paris: OECD, 2001), Table 3–25, p. 157. In a longer framework, the GDP per capita growth rate estimated for the Russian Federation during the period 1973–1998 declined by –1.49 percent per year. Table A1–D, p. 186.

3 Erick Berglof, Andrei Kunov, Julia Shvets and Ksenia Yudaeva, *The New Political Economy of Russia* (Cambridge, MA: MIT Press, 2003), pp. 10–31; Padma Desai, "Russian Retrospectives on Reform from Yeltsin to Putin," *Economic Perspectives* (2005), vol. 19, no. 1, pp. 87–106; Sergei Guriev and Andrei Rachinsky, "The Role of Oligarchs in Russian Capitalism," *Economic Perspectives* (Winter 2005), vol. 19, no. 1, pp. 131–158; and Andrei Schleifer and Daniel Treisman, "A Normal Country: Russia after Communism," *Economic Perspectives* (Winter 2005), vol. 19, no. 1, pp. 169–171; Jacques Sapir, "Russia's Economic Growth and European Integration," *Post-Soviet Affairs* (January–March 2003), vol. 19, no. 1, pp. 1–23.

4 Cf. data in Appendix III, Figure 5 and Figure 7. During the period 1990–1994, Russia experienced hyperinflation, with the annual rate of change in consumer prices at 929.8 percent; from 1994 to 1998 it was still 61.5 percent. *European Bank for Reconstruction and Development (EBRD) Transition Report 1999* (1999) (London, p. 76).

5 Data provided by Russian authorities. On the base of December 1995 = 100, comparable results are provided for the real trade-weighted exchange rate of the ruble: the index for the entire year 1995 = 82.4 and for 1997 = 104.4.

Russian–European Centre for Economic Policy, *Russian Economic Trends* (Moscow, 2001, vol. 10, no. 2, Table D30, p. 105).

6 State Customs Committee, "Russian Federation: Composition of Merchandise Exports, 1994–1999," Moscow, 2000.

7 Ibid.

8 State Data Committee, "Export Windfall Calculation, 1995–2000," based on data provided by Russian authorities and IMF staff estimates for 2000 H1.

9 OECD, *Economic Survey: Russian Federation 1997*. Prepared under the supervision of Sylvana Malle (Paris, 1998), Table A12, p. 257.

10 Ibid.

11 The nominal and real effective exchange rates were estimated with a weighted average of the exchange rates of Russia's main trading partners. OECD, *Economic Survey 2001–2002* (Paris, 2002), Fig. 14, p. 63. See also IMF, Russian Federation: Selected Issues and Statistical Appendix, Washington, DC (April 2002), Country Report No. 02-75, Appendix Table 3, p. 36; European Centre for Economic Policy, *Russian Economic Trends* (Moscow 2002, No. 3). Real wages collapsed as a result of the crisis and remained 60 percent below the pre-crisis level as of the end of 1999.

12 IMF, *Report on the Russian Federation*, September 1, 2000. The growth in most non-industrial sectors was also substantial: agricultural output increased by 4 percent in 1999 and by 8 percent in 2000, continuing to record strong growth in 2001. Orders for tractors and machinery increased by 50 percent in 2000. OECD, *Economic Surveys*, 2001–2002, p. 32. (Labor productivity in industry and construction rose substantially from 1998 to 2000 and even at a more rapid rate from 2000 to 2002. See Figure II.2.)

13 IMF, *Russian Federation, Selected Issues and Statistical Appendix*, Country Report, No. 02–75 (Washington, DC: 2002), Appendix, Table 2, p. 5.

14 Goskomstat.

15 IMF, *Russian Federation, Selected Issues and Statistical Appendix*, Table 15, p. 36.

16 The Economist Intelligence Unit, Russia, Country Report, December 2004, p. 5.

17 It has been claimed that the gas monopoly, Gazprom, sold gas to Russian industrial customers at a sixth of the price it charged European buyers. *Financial Times*, October 19/October 20, 2002, p. 5. According to the World Bank, these price differentials have been exaggerated.

18 On a base of 1997 = 100, seasonally adjusted, Russia's fuel output stood at an index of 96.7 in 1998 H2, and at an index of 98.8 in 1999 H1. The rapid expansion began in 2000 H2, when the index reached 106.4 and rose further to 113.0 by 2001 Q3. OECD, *Economic Surveys*, 2001–2002, Table 3, p. 3. While the average annual growth rate in oil production from 2000 to 2003 was 8.5 percent, the sharp rise in world oil prices in 2004 further increased Russia's oil growth rate to 9.0 percent. But in 2005 the growth rate fell to 2.5 percent. The Economist Intelligence Unit, Russia, Country Report, March 2006, p. 32.

19 IMF, *Russian Federation, Selected Issues and Statistical Appendix*, Table 30, p. 36.

20 Vladimir Putin, *First Person* (New York: Public Affairs, 2001), p. 204 (italics supplied). There were many political parties in the Duma, but the only really big party with a strong social base was the Communist Party, albeit as Putin noted, "one infected with roaches" (ibid., p. 181). He believed that it would

have been extremely difficult to pass any significant legislation without the support of the Communist Party. Therefore, to initiate a program of politico-economic stabilization, the building of pragmatic coalitions was indispensable. Putin affirmed, however, that his leadership would be based on the fundamental principles of developing Russia into a truly democratic, efficiently managed market economy (ibid., pp. 179–187).

21 Controlling inflation thus remains a serious problem. For Russia's CPI, 1995–2002 Q2, see Russian–European Centre for Economic Policy, *Russian Economic Trends* (Moscow, 2002), No. 4, Table D13, p. 88. The percentage change in the CPI, January 1998–December 2001, month on month, is provided in IMF, *Russian Federation, Selected Issues and Statistical Appendix*, Table 15, p. 20. For an annual rate over the period 2000–2005, see Appendix I and Appendix V, infra.

22 IMF, *Russian Federation, Selected Issues and Statistical Appendix*, Table 20, p. 25.

23 Appendix I, infra.

24 Goskomstat, World Bank, and Appendices II.1 and II.2, infra.

25 On a base of December 1995=100, the real value of the ruble, in terms of the U.S. dollar, appreciated from an index of 53.9 for 1999 to an index of 66.6 for 2002 Q2. This, of course, was a significant appreciation at the time, though it was still much lower than the index of 100.5 for the year before the crisis or the index of 84.8 for 1998.

26 Defined as the sum of *final* purchases – which is known as demand-side method estimation and happens to be the method officially favored in most, but not all, nations – the GDP finds textbook expression in the accounting definition: GDP equals C (consumption) plus I (investment) plus G (government purchases) plus X (exports) minus M (imports). Since domestic expenditure is defined as GDP minus $(X - M)$, a more rapid rate of increase in domestic expenditure than in GDP indicates a more rapid rate of increase in domestic expenditure than in the trade balance $(X - M)$.

27 EBRD, *Transition Report 2002* (London, 2002), especially Chapter 2, "Progress in Transaction and the Business Environment." A strong sign of progress in the environment was indicated by the fact that 30-year bonds, which yielded 70 percent in 1998 and 27.5 percent in 1999, yielded 8.4 percent in February 2003 – only 3.6 percentage points higher than U.S. treasuries of comparable maturity.

28 *New York Times* (February 15, 2003), pp. 1–3.

29 In mid-February 2003, British Petroleum made one of the largest foreign direct investments in the Russian energy sector, which was worth \$6.75 billion. This was followed by a \$1.75 billion Gazprom bond in late February – the largest corporate issue at the time in the emerging markets. Heavily subscribed at its launch, the Gazprom ten-year bond traded at 102.5 percent of its face value, at a yield of 9.62 percent, about 200 basis points more than the yield on Russia's sovereign bonds. *New York Times*, August 30, 2003, p. B3.

30 In 2000, Gazprom, in which the government then held a 38 percent stake, was seen as one of Russia's worst-run conglomerates, marred by asset stripping and the disregard for the rights of minority investors. Its reputation has improved under the management of a new chairman installed by President Putin in 2001.

31 Pekka Sutela, "Will Growth in Russia Continue?" *Bank of Finland Bulletin* (2005), vol. 4, p. 18.

32 "Original text of Putin's Annual News Conference for International Journalists," *BBC Monitoring*, Moscow, January 31, 2006, pp. 2, 3–34, 41–44.

33 Vladimir V. Putin, "Energy Egotism Is a Road to Nowhere," *Wall Street Journal*, February 28, 2006, p. A16.

34 The North European Gas Pipeline Company plans to develop the Yuzhno-Russkoye gas field in western Siberia primarily to feed the expanding west European market. This field is expected to yield 22–25 billion cubic meters of gas per year. Gazprom and at least five designated partners are also planning to develop the huge Shtokmanskoye field adjoining the Barents Sea. This deposit is estimated to yield 90 billion cubic meters of gas per year for about 50 years. It will feed not only the European market, but also that of the United States. The BG Group, which is the largest supplier of liquefied natural gas in the United States, expects to acquire gas from the Shtokmanskoye field and market it in liquefied form in the United States, United Kingdom and Spain. The Russian government believes that the Shtokman field could greatly enhance American energy security, providing an opportunity to appropriately align U.S.–Russian relations. *Financial Times*, April 24, 2006, p. 2.

35 Op. cit., "Putin's Annual News Conference for International Journalists," January 31, 2006, p. 15.

2 Transitional constraints

1 "Full text of Putin's annual State-of-the-Nation address to Russian Parliament," Moscow, April 26, 2002, p. 4. The data in the text referred to 2002; at the time of writing (Spring 2007), the situation had not appreciably changed.

2 Vladimir Putin, *First Person*, p. 182. Sergai Y. Yitsin, a professor of law and deputy chairman of President Putin's advisory commission on the judiciary, said recently, "Russian justice has made enormous progress in amending its Soviet-era laws, but is still struggling to overcome deeply ingrained attitudes through all ranks of society that expect the law to be subservient to politics." "Legal Consciousness," he continued, "can only be changed gradually; it's an evolutionary process." *New York Times*, June 20, 2004, p. WK 3. Misconceptions about the operation of a market system are also a discernible phenomenon among some officials, hindering government economic policy and inducing corruption. A provocative analysis of "Misconceptions and Political Outcomes" is presented by David Romer, *Economic Journal* (January 2003), vol. 13, no. 484, pp. 1–20.

3 A careful synthesis of the general literature on corruption is presented in Susan Rose-Ackerman, *Corruption and Government: Causes, Consequences and Reform* (New York: Cambridge University Press, 1999). Relevant specialized studies include Alexander Gurov, *Professional "Naia Prestupnost"* [Crime as Profession] (Moscow, 1990); Gregory Grossman, "Subverted Sovereignty: Historic Role of the Soviet Underground," in *The Tunnel at the End of the Light*, Eds. Stephen S. Cohen and Andrew Schwarz (Berkeley: University of California Press, 1998), pp. 24–50; Robert E. Klitgard, *Controlling Corruption* (Berkeley: University of California Press, 1998); Arindam Das-Gupta and Dilip Mookherjee, *Incentives and Institutional Reforms in Tax Enforcement: An Analysis of Developing Country Experience* (Delhi: Oxford University Press, 1998); Gerard Roland, *Transition and Economics* (Cambridge: MIT Press, 2000), which contains an analysis and bibliography of the periodical literature and empirical evid-

ence on corruption, esp. pp. 171–194; Ya. I. Kuzminov, S.V. Stepashin, J. Roaf, G.A. Satarov and M.I. Levin, papers delivered "On Corruption: A Conference and Seminar on Investment Climate in Russia's Economic Strategy," Moscow, April 5–7, 2000, www.imf.org/external/pubs/ft/ seminar/2000/invest/index.htm; and Andrei Schleifer and Daniel Treisman, "A Normal Country: Russia after Communism," *Economic Perspectives* (Winter 2005), vol. 19, no. 1, pp. 169–171.

4 See Grigory Yavlinsky, "Reforms that Corrupted Russia," *Financial Times*, September 3, 2003, p. 13. Yavlinsky's use of the concept "primary accumulation of capital" had its origins in Marx's discussion on the "primitive accumulation of capital," which denoted the accumulation of capital before the industrial stage of capitalism. Its relevance to privatization is probably Marx's discussion on the enclosure movement of the time, dispossessing agricultural laborers from their tools and the land. As for always being a "crime," Marx speaks of "treachery, bribery, greed and tyranny" as being the exploitation methods of the time. Karl Marx, *Capital* (New York: The Modern Library, 1906), p. 824, pp. 784–804, 822–837; Ross Thomson, "Primitive Capitalist Accumulation," in *Marxian Economics, The New Palgrave*, eds. John Eatwell, Murray Milgate and Peter Newman (New York: W.W. Norton, 1990), pp. 313–320. Mr. Yavlinsky was leader of Yabloko, which, like other opposition parties to the Kremlin, received financial support from Russian businesses. To what he has said on this issue, it should be added that distinguished Western economists have also erred in applying economic concepts applicable to a competitive market economy to conditions of collusive oligopoly. See, e.g., the reference in Vladimir Putin, *First Person*, p. 192.

5 World Bank, *Global Development Finance* (Washington, DC, 2000), pp. 186–187. Russian state property was not offered for sale to foreigners, which was another factor for the relatively low government receipts from privatization.

6 EBRD, *Transition Report 1999* (London, 1999), pp. 110–111. The Gini coefficient ranges from 0 to 1; at 0 everyone has the same income and at 1 only one person has all the income. According to Goskomstat data, Russia's Gini coefficient rose from 0.26 in 1991 to 0.41 in 1994 and stabilized thereafter at about 0.40 through the end of the decade. A study for the World Bank attributes 77 percent of the increase to the growing dispersion of wage incomes. (Branko Milanovic, "Explaining the Growth in Income Inequality During the Transition," *World Bank* (Washington, DC, 1998), p. 22. See also Schleifer and Treisman, op. cit., pp. 159–162. In 1991, the income ratio between the most affluent 10 percent and the poorest 10 percent was 4:1; by 1995, the ratio was 13.5:1 (and if we include illegal activity, it was 25:1). *Vlast* (Moscow, November 11, 1995), p. 42, and *Izvestia* (Moscow, February 14, 1996) as cited in Georgii Arbatov, "Origins and Consequences of Shock Therapy," in *The New Russia: Transition Gone Awry*, Eds. Lawrence R. Klein and Marshall Pomer (Stanford, CA: Stanford University Press, 2001), p. 175. For an expert analysis of the related demographic catastrophe of the 1990s (e.g. in Russia, male life expectancy at birth fell from 64.2 years in 1989 to 47.6 years in 1994), see Elizabeth Brainerd and David M. Cutler, "Autopsy on an Empire: Understanding Mortality in Russia and the Former Soviet Union," *Economic Perspectives* (Winter 2005), vol. 19, no. 1, pp. 107–130.

7 Yavlinsky, op. cit. "Reforms that Corrupted Russia."

8 Report. On the work of scholar/mathematician Georgii A. Satarov in Sabrina Tavernis, "A Russian Tilts at Graft," *New York Times*, February 16, 2003, p. A3.
9 *Financial Times*, August 8, 2003, p. 12; August 18, 2003, p. 9. For a summary of empirical studies on privatization in Russia and former Soviet republics, see William L. Megginson and Jeffry M. Netter, "From State to Market: A Survey of Empirical Studies on Privatization," *Journal of Economic Literature* (June 2001), vol. 39, no. 2, Table 7, p. 362 and sources cited on p. 363. The survey by the World Bank was based on a sampling of 1,300 companies and concludes that Russia's 23 largest business groups control more than a third of its industry by sales. *Financial Times*, April 7, 2004, p. 4. For a careful synthesis of the data, see Sergei Guriev and Andrei Rachinsky, "The Role of Oligarchs in Russian Capitalism," *Economic Perspectives* (Winter 2005), vol. 19, no. 1, pp. 131–149.
10 Full text of Putin's annual State-of-the-Nation address to Russian parliament (Moscow, April 26, 2002), p. 3.
11 *New York Times*, May 13, 2006, p. A6; *Financial Times*, June 4, 2006, p. 1.
12 Ibid. Italics supplied.
13 See Satarov, op. cit., "A Russian Tilts at Graft," and papers "On Corruption," by Ya. I. Kuzminov and G.A. Satarov (Moscow, April 5–7, 2000).

3 Basic principles toward a successful Russian market economy

1 I am indebted to Alan Greenspan and James Tobin, who commented on these issues while visiting Berkeley. See Alan Greenspan, address delivered at the Annual Business Faculty Research Dialog, University of California, Berkeley, September 9, 1998, pp. 4–7, and his stimulating paper on "International Imbalance," The Advancing Enterprise Consonance, London, England, 2005, pp. 1–13; James Tobin, "False Expectations," in *The New Russia: Transition Gone Awry*, Lawrence R. Klein and Marshall Pomer (Stanford, CA: Stanford University Press, 2001), pp. 28–34.
2 Professor Charles H. Townes, University of California, Berkeley, September 3, 1998. For a related, provocative paper dealing with the origin of quantum electronics, the laser, practical uses and the problem of research planning, see Charles H. Townes, "Quantum Electronics and Surprise in Development of Technology," *Science* (February 16, 1968), vol. 159, no. 3816, esp. pp. 699–701. See also Townes, oral history transcript entitled *Charles Hard Townes, A Life in Physics, Bell Telephone Laboratories and World War II, Columbia University and the Laser, MIT and Government Service, California and Research in Astrophysics* (Regional Oral History Office, Bancroft Library, 1994), esp. p. 204. Townes and the Soviet physicists – Dr. Nikolai Gennadievich Basov and Dr. Alexander Mekhailovich Prochorov – who independently and simultaneously discovered the maser and the laser – shared the Nobel Prize in physics in 1964. See the fascinating essay on those discoveries by B. Edlin in *Les Prix Nobel En 1964* (Stockholm, 1965), pp. 23–25 and the papers by the three nobelists, pp. 99–156.
3 Zh. I. Alferov, "The History and Future of Semiconductor Heterostructures from the Point of View of a Russian Scientist," *Physica Scripta* (1996), vol. T68, pp. 33, 42. See also Gerber and Deborah Yarsike Ball, "The State of Russian Science: Focus Groups with Nuclear Physicists," *Post-Soviet Affairs* (2002) vol. 18, no. 3, pp. 183–212, and sources cited therein.

4 John R. Whinnery, "Lasers for Optical Communication," *The Froelich/Kent Encyclopedia of Telecommunications, Volume 10* (New York: Marcel Dekker, Inc., 1995), pp. 228–229.

5 For company and other non-Federal funds for industrial R&D performance in the United States as a percentage of net sales of enterprises that performed industrial R&D in the United States by industry and size of company (1997–2000), see National Science Foundation, *Research and Development in Industry 2000* (Washington, DC, 2001), Table A–20. For all industries, the figure in 2000 was 3.4; for chemicals, 5.0; pharmaceuticals and medicines, 9.8; computer and electronic products, 8.5; professional scientific and technical services, 14.9 – of which scientific R&D services equalled 32.3; and small manufacturing companies, 40.8.

6 When discussing this issue, all Russian economists interviewed by the author stressed the urgent need for the Russian government to expand expenditures on R&D. A comparison of the available data shows that for total national R&D expenditures, as a percentage of GDP, in 1999, the record was as follows:

United States	2.82
Japan	3.01
Germany	2.38
France	2.17
United Kingdom	1.87
Italy	1.04

The Russian government's total national expenditure on R&D as a percentage of GDP appears to be considerably less than 0.5 percent. European Commission, *Russian Economic Trends* (Moscow, 2002), Table E8, p. 878, and IMF, *Russian Federation: Selected Issues* (Washington, DC: September 1, 2000), Table 23, p. 80, on references in terms of various categories of R&D as a percentage of government expenditures.

4 Policy reforms for the longer term

1 The Russian government has established a Fiscal Stabilization Fund. Though this section was prepared prior to this fund, I am pleased to find that where we are dealing with the same issues, the goals of the fund and my proposal are similar. However, as will be shown, the goals of the Fiscal Fund are more limited and some of the provisions subject to serious misuse.

2 For an applicable discussion on the impact of fiscal policy on output and on the right measure of fiscal policy, see Alan J. Auerbach, "Fiscal Policy, Past and Present," *Brookings Papers on Economic Activity* (Washington, DC: November 1, 2003), esp. pp. 114–121; Gauti Eggertsson and Michael Woodford, "The Zero Bound on Interest Rates and Optimal Monetary Policy," *Brookings Papers on Economic Activity* (Washington, DC: November 1, 2003), esp. pp. 198–207. [On April 23, 2004, the Duma approved a legislation raising "natural resource taxes for oil exports." The tax will increase with the rise in the international price of oil. If the price of oil stays between $20 and $25 a barrel, export duties would increase from 35 to 45 percent of the difference between $20 and the actual price of oil. If the price of oil rises above $25 a barrel, this marginal duty will increase from 45 to 65 percent of the difference between $25 and the actual oil price. The tax will decrease if the price

of oil falls below $20 a barrel. (*Financial Times*, March 23, 2004, p. 6; April 24/25, 2004, p. 2.)]

3 In April 2001, the Russian government and the CBR issued a joint document including provisions "to stimulate the engagement of the banking sector in the modernization of the national economy." The CBR, it continued, "undertook to come up with sensible ways for Central Bank withdrawal from the assets of the banks in which it was present during the source of its development." *Russian Government, Central Bank Approved Joint Statement on Economy* (BBC Monitoring, London, April 2001). But little was accomplished. In March 2002, President Putin appointed a new expert governor for the CBR. For a synthesis of the history and reasons for the failure to reform the banking system, see Koen Schoors, *The Fate of Russia's Former State Banks: Chronicle of a Restructuring Postponed and a Crisis Foretold* (Certse: Ghent University, 2001). Significantly, many "spontaneous privatizations" of the state banks occurred before 1992 under bad laws and bad economic conditions. Further, in the 1990s, oligarchs often transferred deposits from de facto insolvent subsidiaries to parent banks, mostly leaving liabilities to the receiver. With about 1,300 licensed banks, many of which are operating at the minimum capital requirements of $1.2 million – an absurdly low figure – a systematic restructuring of Russia's fragmented banking system is overdue. For improvements in Russia's banking structure: S. Claeys *et al.* "Bank Supervision Russian Style: Rules versus Enforcement and Tacit Objective" William Davidson Institute Working Papers Series wp 778, University of Michigan, 2005)
4 World Bank, Country Department, *Russia: Economic Report* (Washington, DC, February 2004), Table 5, p. 8.
5 For considerable data on the improvement in the financial markets, see *Russian Economic Trends* (Moscow, No. 401, June 2003), prepared by Lyubov Loukashova, Sergei Nikolaenko, Andrei Polatayev and Vladimir Redkin; the editor-in-chief is Andrei Shastitko.
6 *New York Times*, November 1, 2003, pp. B1, B15.
7 *Financial Times*, November 22, 2003, p. 8.
8 *Financial Times*, November 9, 2003, p. 6.
9 For widely varied views on this issue, cf. *Financial Times*, November 1, 2003, pp. W1, W2; *New York Times*, November 3, 2003, p. A3 and November 9, pp. WK1, WK5; *Wall Street Journal*, November 17, 2003, p. A20; and *New York Review*, December 4, 2003, p. 28, columns 3–5.
10 *New York Times*, November 3, 2003, p. A3.
11 Ibid.
12 According to the World Bank, after a net inflow of private capital in the first half of 2003, the country witnessed a net outflow from July to mid-November (*New York Times*, November 15, 2003, p. A3). Later data show, however, that for the two months of August and September CBR foreign exchange reserves fell by $2.5 billion, and they rose by about $3 billion in October to a total of $64.9 billion. Russia was also attracting more and more foreign capital, a total of $21 billion during the period January–September 2003, an increase of 62 percent on the year-over-year basis (L.R. Klein and V. Eskin, "Current Quarter Model of the Russian Economy," University of Pennsylvania, November 2003, pp. 1–2.
13 *New York Times*, November 15, 2003, p. A3.
14 *Financial Times*, November 6, 2003, p. 3.

15 Putin, *First Person*, p. 196.

16 Ibid.

17 Review of *George Bush and Brent Scowcroft, A World Transformed* (New York, Alfred A. Knopf, 1998), by Fareed Zakaria, *New York Times Book Review*, September 21, 1998, p. 10.

18 In 2002, Russia's global proportion of GDP was 2.7 percent and of world exports and imports only 1.6 percent, IMF, *World Economic Outlook* (Washington, DC, April 2003), p. 161. These proportions were higher than those in the year before the 1998 crisis: in 1997 they were 1.9 percent for GDP and 1.5 percent for exports and imports of goods and services.

19 EBRD, "Transcript of the Launch of the Transition Report 2003" (Brussels, no. 2003), statement by Professor Willem Buiter, pp. 14–15.

20 A guide to WTO law and practice is provided in *WTO Analytical Index* (Lanham, MD: Berhan Press, 2003), 2 vols.

21 For a synthesis of this literature, see Paul R. Krugman and Maurice Obstfeld, *International Economics* (Glencoe, IL: Foresman and Co., 2003), pp. 120–157; Elanan Helpman, "The Structure of Foreign Trade," *Economic Perspectives* (Spring 1999), vol. 13, no. 2, pp. 121–144; Pol Antros, "Firms, Contracts, and Trade Structure," *Quarterly Journal of Economics* (November 2003), vol. 123, esp. pp. 1402–1411, where it is shown that "overall the significant effect of the capital–labor ratio of the exporting country on the share of intrafirm imports appears to be robust," p. 1409; and John M Letiche, ed., *International Economic Policies and Their Theoretical Foundations* (San Diego, CA: Academic Press, Inc., 1992), pp. 80–84.

22 According to Russian experts, this is particularly the case in electronics. Russian scientific labs have an abundance of specialists in very high-density components on chips, optoelectronics, specialized lasers and high-speed transistors. The distribution of Russia's foreign trade would also be complementary to its economic diversification. About 51 percent of Russia's commodity exports are sold to developed economies and 49 percent to developing ones – OECD, *International Trade by Commodity Statistics* (Paris, 2002), p. 394. While Russia's exports to the EU as a proportion of its total exports have recently been about 36 percent, with the enlargement of the EU from 15 to 25 countries that occurred in May 2004, Russia's two-way trade with the EU is projected to comprise about 50 percent of its total foreign trade. Russia's exports of goods and services to the United States as a proportion of its total exports have been only about 6 percent, but most projections suggest that an expanding match could be developed between the supply of Russia's oil and gas reserves, as well as higher-valued goods and services, and U.S. high-tech/information-technology exportables. For projections on Russia's exports of oil and gas to the EU, the United States and to the rest of the world for the period 2003–2030, see International Energy Agency, *World Energy Outlook* (Paris 2004). See also *Financial Times*, October 13, 2004, p. 1; October 21, p. 27; and October 27, p. 6.

5 The Yukos crisis

1 *Financial Times*, November 7, 2003, p. 5; *New York Times*, November 15, 2003, p. 3.

2 Detailed coverage of the Yukos crisis appeared in the public press during July and August 2003, e.g. (i) *Financial Times*, July 4, 2003, p. 12; July 10, p. 4;

July 19, p. 4; July 24, p. W1; July 27, p. 7; July 29, p. 3; July 30, p. 3; July 31, p. 9; August 4, pp. 13–14; August 8, p. A9; August 11, p. 2; August 15, p. 5; (ii) *New York Times*, July 8, 2003, pp. W1, W7; July 18, pp. W1, W7; July 24, pp. W1, W7; August 8, p. 9.

3 *New York Times*, July 18, 2003, pp. W1, W7; August 8, p. A9. In an interview on September 20, 2003, President Putin reiterated that as president he could not interfere with the independence of prosecutors, who were simply upholding the law. "Nobody," he emphasized, "can be free from complying with the law, even those who have amassed billions." Furthermore, he dismissed accusations of Kremlin involvement or political interference in the Yukos matter as "utter nonsense." *New York Times*, September 2, 2003, p. 5.

4 World Bank Database.

5 *Financial Times*, August 15, 2003, p. 5.

6 Comprehensive coverage of the October–November Yukos "crisis" appeared in the Western press, e.g. (i) *Financial Times*, October 21, 2003, pp. 1, 4; October 28, pp. 1, 3; October 29, p. 4; October 30, p. 4; October 31, pp. 1, 4; November 2, pp. 1, 3, W2; November 3, pp. 13, 17, 27; November 4, pp. 24, 25; November 5, p. 1; November 6, p. 13; November 7, p. 5; November 9, p. 6; November 11, pp. 4, 10, 16, 24; November 12, p. 6; November 13, p. 2; November 19, p. 4; November 22, p. 8; November 27, p. 22; November 30, pp. 1, 8; (ii) *New York Times*, October 26, 2003, pp. 1, 7, 12; October 31, p. A14; October 31, pp. 1, A5, C4; November 1, pp. 1, A6, B1, B15; November 3, pp. A3, A5; November 4, pp. A3, A11; November 4, pp. A10, A25; November 7, p. A3; November 9, pp. 12, WK1, WK5; November 15, p. A3.

7 For the prosecutors' accusation on this matter at Khodorkovsky's trial, see *Financial Times*, April 27, 2005, p. 2. Russia's statute of limitations applied in this situation and the charges in regard to it were dismissed. It has been claimed, however, that this case concerned tax issues rather than privatization deals. A May 2004 court decision held that those deemed to have known to be illegal in privatization deals can be pursued indefinitely. See William Tompson, "Putting Yukos in Perspective," *Post-Soviet Affairs* (April–June 2005), vol. 21, no. 2, p. 163.

8 (i) *New York Times*, May 20, 2004, pp. W1, W7; May 29, 2004, p. A17; (ii) *Financial Times*, May 21, 2004, p. 3; June 1, 2004, pp. 11, 18; June 2, 2004, p. 28; June 18, 2004, p. 17; June 24, 2004, p. 7; June 25, 2004, p. 25, p. 20.

9 *New York Times*, July 10, 2003, p. B3; July 21, 2004, pp. W1, W7; July 23, 2004, pp. W1, W7. On August 6, a Moscow arbitration court overturned a district court decision and ruled that bailiffs had no legal ground to freeze Yuganskneftegas' shares; *Financial Times*, August 7/8, 2004, p. 9. But on August 9, 2004, the Moscow arbitration court reversed its decision and froze the company's shares; *Financial Times*, August 10, 2004, p. 16; *New York Times*, August 10, 2004, p. C5.

10 *Financial Times*, November 2, 2003, p. 24; Deutsche Bank Trust Company Americas, depositary's notice of extraordinary general meeting of shareholders of Yukos corporation, November 26, 2004.

11 Ibid.

12 *Financial Times*, November 5, 2004, p. 3.

13 *Financial Times*, November 29, 2004, p. 1.

14 *Financial Times*, December 1, 2004, pp. 1, 17.

15 *Financial Times*, December 18/19, 2004, p. 8; December 20, 2004, p. 1.

16 *New York Times*, December 18, 2004, p. A-8.
17 *Financial Times*, December 18/19, 2004, p. 8; December 20, p. 1.
18 *New York Times*, December 20, 2004, pp. 1, A13.
19 *Financial Times*, December 21, 2004, p. 22.
20 See President Putin's interview in Schleswig, Germany, Associated Press, *San Francisco Chronicle*, December 22, 2004, p. 1, C3. For the president's extended comments, see also *New York Times*, December 22, 2004, p. W1; December 24, pp. C1, C3.
21 *Financial Times*, December 23, 2004, p. 1.
22 *Financial Times*, January 7, 2005, p. 15.
23 *Financial Times*, January 2, 2005, p. 10.
24 *Financial Times*, May 18, 2005, p. 12; June 16, 2005, p 16.
25 For deliberations between the companies and the government, see *Financial Times*, September 20, 2004, p. 27; December 10, p. 17; December 29, p. 18; February 26/27, 2005, p. 8; March 3, 2004, p. 19; and May 4, 2005, p. 16.
26 *Financial Times*, May 18, 2005, p. 12.
27 *Financial Times*, October 25, 2005, p. 25.
28 *Financial Times*, April 19, 2006, p. 11.
29 *Financial Times*, March 29, 2006, p. 16.
30 *Financial Times*, May 4, 2006, p. 4; May 31, 2006, p. 2.
31 According to Russia's Federal Statistical Service, the situation improved in April 2005. However, projections for the annual GDP growth rate were revised downward to 5.6 percent – well below the 2004 rate of 7.1 percent. Lawrence R. Klein, Vladimir Eskin and Andrei Roudoi, *Quarterly Model of the Russian Economy* (University of Pennsylvania) and *Global Insight*, April 2005, p. 2; June 2005, p. 1, 2; *Financial Times*, June 21, 2005, p. 4; June 24, p. 9.
32 *New York Times*, November 17, 2004, p. W-1. The roots of the Yukos case, one economist has written, "lie in the very structure of the relationship between business and the state in post-Soviet Russia." Tompson, William, "Putting Yukos in Perspective," *Post-Soviet Affairs* (April–June 2005), vol. 21. This structure, the argument continues, has made it impossible to establish a modus vivendi between big business and the state, allegedly, contributing "instead to a situation in which periodic campaigns of annihilation against prominent businessmen are a regular occurrence." On the contrary, the Yukos affair has been a singular rather than a periodic occurrence. By placing emphasis on political and economic stability, President Putin has been able to constrain the destructive forces of bureaucracy and those of economic pressure groups to prevent further Yukos affairs.
33 Ibid.
34 "Full text of Putin's Annual State of the Nation address to Russian Parliament," Moscow, April 25, 2005; *Financial Times*, April 26, 2005, p. 1.
35 On May 31, 2005, a Russian court convicted Mikhail Khodorkovsky on criminal charges and sentenced him to nine years in prison. His business partner, Platon Lebedev, was similarly convicted and sentenced. Khodorkovsky was found guilty by a panel of judges on six of seven charges ranging from fraud and embezzlement to corporate and personal tax evasion. The court also ordered the two men to pay $613 million in taxes and fines. Although Khodorkovsky will be eligible for release in 2012, Russia's prosecutor-general said that his office was preparing new money-laundering charges against both men. On June 9, 2005, Khodorkovsky's lawyers called on the Moscow City Court to overturn the verdict

and the nine-year prison sentence. *Financial Times*, June 1, 2005, p. 1; *New York Times*, June 1, 2005, pp. 1, 10A; June 2, p. C6; June 10, p. A6. On September 22, 2005, the Moscow City Court denied the appeal. However, the sentence was reduced from nine to eight years. *Financial Times*, September 23, 2005, p. 2.

36 On February 25, 2007, Russia's prosecuters brought new charges of embezzlement and money laundering against Khodorkovsky and Lebedev amounting to about $20 billion; these charges could carry sentences of 15 years. *Financial Times*, February 6, 2007, p. 4; *New York Times*, February 6, 2007, p. 4-10. In government auctions and via bilateral deals, Gazprom and Rosneft have acquired a substantial proportion of the remaining Yukos assets. *New York Times*, April 5, 2007, p. C-3; *Financial Times*, April 5, 2007, p. C-3.

6 Transitional tensions and permanent interests

1 EBRD, "Transcript of the Launch of the Transition Report 2003," London, p. 15.

2 *Financial Times*, September 20, 2003, p. 2. Russia complained, furthermore, that the enlargement of the EU in 2004 seriously affects the status of the Conventional Forces in Europe (CFE) Treaty, negotiated between NATO and the Warsaw Pact in the 1980s, signed in Paris in 1997 and updated at Istanbul in 1999. The objective of the treaty was to reduce conventional armed forces in Europe and is regarded by Western countries as a bulwark of European security. In February 2004, the Russian Minister of Defense said that his government would not ratify the treaty in its existing form, because it stipulated that there would be no substantial deployment of conventional forces close to Russian borders, whereas the enlargement process would negate these terms – particularly in the Baltic States and in Poland. The EU took the position that some concessions to Russia may be justified, but failure to ratify the treaty would be a deleterious setback to EU–Russian relations. *Financial Times*, February 23, 2004, p. 2; February 25, 2004, p. 12; February 26, 2004, p. 13; and March 11, 2004, p. 2. The United States has declared that it plans to establish anti-missile facilities in the Czech Republic and Poland, which have exacerbated the controversy.

3 *Financial Times*, February 23, 2004, p. 2; February 24, 2004, p. 13.

4 *Financial Times*, February 25, 2004, p. 12.

5 *Wall Street Journal*, May 25, 2005, Sec. B, p. 2.

6 Since the Soviet era, Russia has retained military bases in Georgia and in Trans Dnestr, a region in Moldova, controlled by Russian nationalists who are seeking autonomy from Moldova. In 1999, Russia made a commitment to complete withdrawal of its forces in a timely way from Adzharia, a separatist province of Georgia, but has not yet done so. While the President of Georgia, Mikhail Sakashvili, had the U.S. government's backing and its pledge of security for Georgia in the Caucusus, the governor of the separatist province of Adzharia, Asian Abashidze, had the backing of Russia. In early March 2004, Sakashvili was prevented from holding a rally in Adzharia, and he declared this action amounted to armed revolt. In consequence, on March 14, 2004, he imposed an economic blockade of Batumi, the capital of Adzharian traders. Abashidze responded by threatening to send his troops into the streets. The United States and Russia made it unambiguously clear that they would not interfere in the conflict, precluding a crisis that could have jeopardized their mutual interests in

combating terrorism in the area. The economic blockade of Batumi lasted only four days; the leaders of Georgia and Adzharia met and declared that their *imminent* differences were resolved. However, in April 2004, Georgia launched military exercises 70 kilometers off the Adzharia border and demanded that Abashidze should immediately resign. On May 5, 2004, he fled to Moscow. Shortly thereafter Sakashvili announced that he would pursue a foreign policy binding Georgia to western Europe. Russia has said it will withdraw its troops from Georgia by 2008. The economic and security objectives of the region as well as those of Russia and the United States would be well served if the following two integrating agreements aimed at freeing foreign trade and investment among the nations and opening their economies globally were fully implemented and extended: (1) the agreement between Georgia, Ukraine, Uzbekistan, Azerbaijan and Moldova (GUUAM), founded in 1997; and (2) the agreement between Russia, Belarus, Kazakhstan, the Kyrgyz Republic and Tajikistan – established as the Eurasian Economic Community (EAEC) in 2000. See European Central Bank, "Economic Integration in Selected Regions outside the European Union," *Monthly Bulletin* (Frankfurt, October 2004), pp. 67–70; and Michael Rywkin, "Putin and Russia's Southern Belt since the Iraq War," *American Foreign Policy Interests*, 2004, vol. 26, pp. 11–19. *Financial Times*, November 12, 2003, p. 6; February 23, 2004, p. 2; February 25, 2004, p. 12; March 3, 2004, p. 2; March 15, 2004, p. 2; July 2, 2004, p. 6; October 19, 2004, p. 17. *New York Times*, November 27, 2003, p. A-16; December 6, 2003, p. A-6; February 9, p. A-2; March 15, 2004, p. A-8; April 3, 2004, pp. A-3, A-7; May 6, 2004, p. 6; October 12, 2004, p. 8; October 15, p. 14; November 14, 2004, p. WK-3, p. 6. At time of writing, the controversy between Russia and Georgia remains unresolved

7 *New York Times*, January 26, 2004, pp. A-1, A-10.

8 *New York Times*, January 27, 2004, p. A-3.

9 See Andrew Jack, "Russia and the EU Agree to Terms with WTO Entry," *Financial Times*, May 22/23, 2004, p. 5; Guy Chazan, "EU Backs Russia's WTO Entry as Russia Supports Kyoto Pact," *Wall Street Journal*, May 22, 2004, pp. A-2, A-6; Erin Aredlund, "Europe Backs Russian Entry into WTO," *New York Times*, May 22, 2004, pp. B-1, B-3. On May 16, 2005, Russia and the EU signed an agreement on diplomatic cooperation, focusing on such issues as integrating Russia's laws with EU's competitive policies, intellectual property rights, textile and pharmaceutical sectors. The two sides pledged to cooperate in removing barriers to trade, jointly fighting terrorism, proliferation of weapons, organized crime and adopting uniform educational standards. *Financial Times*, May 11, 2005, p. 2; *New York Times*, May 11, 2005, p. A-3.

10 *New York Times*, May 22, 2004, p. B-3. On November 19, 2006, the U.S. and Russia signed a far-reaching commercial agreement, signaling Russia's entry into the WTO. For terms of the agreement, see Document SNS 00000 2006 1122 e2BK 0000I usinfo.state/gov.

11 Statement by Junichiro Koizumy, Japan's prime minister, *Financial Times*, April 30/May 1, 2005, p. 2. See also the discussion by Kiyoshi Kojima on "Asian Economic Integration for the 21st Century," in *The Flying Geese Theory of Economic Development* (Tokyo, 2004), pp. 300–329; and M. Dutta, "Asian Economic Community: Intra-community Macro- and Micro-Economic Parameters," *Journal of Asian Economics* (July–August 2002), vol. 13.4.

12 *Financial Times*, September 11, 2004, p. 19; September 22, p. 6; September

23, p. 21; October 3, p. 1; December 27, 2004, p. 1; January 4, 2005, p. E1; January 8/9, pp. 1, 8; January 14, p. 17; *New York Times*, September 28, 2004, p. W-1; December 31, p. W-7.

13 *New York Times*, January 15, 2005, p. B-3; *Financial Times*, January 16, p. 8.

14 See "Nobel Laureate North Argues Institutions Have Crucial Role in Economic Growth," IMF Survey, vol. 31, no. 11 (June 10, 2002), pp. 191–192; and EBRD, "Transcript of the Launch of the Transition Report 2003," pp. 5–21.

15 In the United States, it has been the communications media, rather than the government, that originally has called attention to the egregious corruption of companies such as ENRON. The experience of the United States also suggests that the controversies between "censorship" and "irresponsible" reporting could productively be considered in an evolutionary context with the establishment of an independent Federal Communications Commission in Russia.

16 See President Putin's presidential statement and inaugural address: www.putin2004.ru; and encouraging commentaries made by cabinet ministers whom he appointed for his second term in office. *New York Times*, February 17, 2004, p. A-6; March 3, 2004, p. A-26; March 6, 2004, p. A-3; March 23, 2004, p. A-26; *Financial Times*, March 3, 2004, p. 4.

17 Boris Yeltsin, "We will not deviate from the spirit and the letter of the constitution," and Mikhail Gorbachev, "This actually is a retreat from democracy," *Moskovskiye Novosti*, September 17, 2004. See also *Financial Times*, September 14, 2004, pp. 4–6, 12; September 16, p. 2; *New York Times*, September 14, 2004, pp. 1, A-8; September 19, sec. 4, pp. WK, 1, 7, 12; September 15, pp. 1, A-8.

18 The constitutional amendments were scheduled for late 2005 or early 2006. The newly elected president will largely control the Foreign Ministry, the Ministry of Defense and the federal intelligence services. He will also appoint the regional governors. But the parliament will form a majority coalition that will choose a prime minister, all the other ministers and the heads of the government boards. The prime minister will, therefore, lead the cabinet of ministers and set the legislative and budgetary agenda. The president will have the power to veto legislation, which could be overturned by a two-thirds majority of the parliament. Among his priorities as president, Yushchenko plans to create a Ministry of European Integration, which would include a cabinet-level post. Nonetheless, he has said: "Russia is a strategic interest to Ukraine in the sphere of economic, humanitarian, military and technical interest. It is our task and the obligation of Ukraine that we resolve all problems with Russia" (*New York Times*, December 31, 2004, p. A-3). As for the Ukraine crisis, see *New York Times*, December 9, 2004, p. 1; *Financial Times*, December 9, 2004, p. 1; October 20, 2004, p. 4; November 24, p. 1; November 26, 2004, p. 1; November 28, pp. 2, 6; November 29, p. 1; November 30, p. 1; December 2, p. 2; December 3, p. 2; December 4/5, p. 1; *New York Times*, November 24, 2004, pp. 1, A-10; November 25, pp. 1, A-10; November 28, pp. 1, 16; November 29, pp. 1, A-16; November 30, pp. 1, A-8, A-12; December 1, p. A-14; December 2, pp. 1, A-14; December 3, pp. 1, A-12; December 4, pp. 1, A-10; December 5, p. 6. For discussions on the unsuccessful administration of President Yushchenko, in part caused by Russia's rise in the price of gas, see *Financial Times*, March 24, 2006, p. 11 and March 27, p. 1; *New York Times*, March 27, 2006, pp. 1, A-6, March 30, p. A-3. After 4 months of political paralysis, on August 3, 2006, President Yushchenko nominated Mr. Yanukovich as prime

minister, which the Ukraine parliament approved the next day. Political instability continued. Viktor Yushchenko, "Ukraine's crisis needs a firm response," *Financial Times*, April 4, 2007, p. 11. *New York Times*, April 4, 2007, p. 11.

19 See Roger B. Myerson, Review of *Incentives and Political Economy*, by Jean-Jacques Laffont. Oxford University Press, 2000, in *Journal of Economic Literature* (December 2001), vol. 39, no. 4, pp. 1277–1279.

20 *Sunday Times*, London, March 26, 2006, p. 25.

21 *New York Times*, June 12, 2006, pp. A-1, A-6.

22 *Financial Times*, March 15, 2006, p. 20; March 31, 2006, p. 1; May 31, 2006, p. 1.

23 *Financial Times*, April 22, 2006, p. C-6.

24 *Financial Times*, May 30, 2006, p. 1.

25 *Financial Times*, June 26, 2006, p. 20.

26 Department of Commerce, *Energy Information Administration*, "International Energy Outlook," Washington, DC, 2006, pp. 1–6. See also Ben S Bernanke, "Energy and Economy," Economic Club of Chicago, Chicago, Illinois, June 15, 2006, pp. 1–6. Gawdat Bahgat, "Europe's energy security: challenges and opportunities," *International Affairs*, 2006, vol. 82, no. 5, 961–975.

27 Nonetheless, the available evidence indicates that the world is not in imminent danger of running out of energy. At the end of 2005, the world proved recoverable resources of crude oil – using existing technologies and under current economic conditions – stood at a 15 percent higher level than a decade earlier. Thus, the current level of oil reserves is equal to about 40 years of global consumption at current rates of utilization. These estimates exclude such factors as the oil sands of Canada, the ongoing increases of efficiency in the use of energy, the expected rise in the use of coal, nuclear energy and bio-fuels.

28 The Russia–Ukraine crisis was comprehensively covered in the press. *Financial Times*, January 3, 2006, p. 1; January 4, 2006, p. 13; January 12, 2006, p. 3; January 17, 2006, p. 2; March 7, 2006, p. 3; March 8, p. 2; April 30, p. 1; May 8, pp. 1, 2. *New York Times*, May 5, 2006, pp. A-1, A-10.

29 *New York Times*, December 31, 2005, p. A-4.

30 Ibid.

31 Under WTO rules, the principles of reciprocity would, of course, be implemented multilaterally and would be consistent with the diversification of energy imports from all member states.

32 *Financial Times*, April 22, 2006, p. C-6.

33 *Financial Times*, May 30, 2006, p. 1.

34 *New York Times*, January 2, 2006, p. 8.

35 Alexey Kaulbars, "Special Report Overview of the Russian Foreign Trade in 2005" in L.R. Klein, V. Eskin and A. Roudoi, "Current Quarter Model of the Russian Economy: Forecast Summary," University of Pennsylvania and Global Insight. March 2006, pp. 3–5.

36 *Financial Times*, June 30, 2006, p. 8. By the end of 2006, comparing year-end levels, the real effective exchange rate of the ruble had appreciated 17 percent and 5.89 percent, respectively, in terms of the U.S. dollar and the euro. Still year-over-year, in 2006 the real GDP growth rate had expanded 6.7 percent. L.R. Klein *et al.* "Current Quarter Model of the Russian Economy: Forecast Summary," University of Pennsylvannia and Prognoz. January 2007, pp. 1–2.

37 *New York Times*, February 22, 2006, p. C-1.

38 See the Symposium on "IT Diffusion and Industry and Labour-Market Dynamics," *Economic Journal* (February 2006), vol. 116, no. 309, pp. F11–F118.

39 Pekka Sutela, "Will Growth in Russia Continue?" *Bank of Finland Bulletin* (November 1, 2005), vol. 79, no. 4, pp. 14–18.

7 Concluding observations

1 Jan de Vries, "Economic Growth Before and After the Industrial Revolution: A Modest Proposal," in *Early Modern Capitalism*, Ed. M. Prak (London: Routledge, 2001), pp. 177–194; "Dutch Economic Growth in Comparative-Historical Perspective, 1500–2000," *De Economist* (2000), vol. 148, no. 4, pp. 443–467, and sources cited therein.

Bibliography

Abalkin, L.I. *et al.* 1999. *Russia-2015: Optimistic Scenario* (Russian Academy of Sciences).

Ades, Alberto and Rafael Di Tella. 1999. "Rents, Competition and Corruption," *American Economic Review*, 89:4, pp. 982–993.

Aghion, P. and O. Blanchard. 1994. "On the Speed of Transition in Central Europe." NBER Working Paper No. 4736.

Aghion, P. and R. Burgess. 1993. "Financing in Eastern Europe and the Former Soviet Union: Issues and Institutional Support," In Ed. Dilip K. Das, *International Finance: Contemporary Issues*, Routledge, pp. 101–124.

Aghion, P., P. Howitt and David Mayer-Foulkes. 2003. "The Effect of Financial Development on Convergence: Theory and Evidence." Mimeo.

Akran, Q. Farooq. 2004. "Oil Prices and Exchange Rates: Norwegian Evidence," *Econometrics Journal*, 7:2, pp. 476–504.

Alexeev, M. 1999. "Privatization and Distribution of Wealth in Russia," *Economics of Transition*, 7, pp. 449–465.

Alferov, Zh I. 1996. "The History and Future of Semiconductor Heterostructures from the Point of View of a Russian Scientist," *Physica Scripta*, T68, pp. 32–45.

Andrienko, Yuri and Sergei Guriev. 2004. "Determinants of Interregional Mobility in Russia," *Economics of Transition*, 12:1, pp. 1–27.

Antros, Pol. 2003. "Firms, Contracts, and Trade Structure," *Quarterly Journal of Economics*, CSV123, pp. 1402–1411.

Aslund, A. 1995. *How Russia Became a Market Economy*, Brookings Institution.

—— 2003. *Building Capitalism*, Cambridge University Press.

Auerbach, Alan J. 2003. "Fiscal Policy, Past and Present," Washington, Brookings Papers on Economic Activity, no. 1, pp. 75–122.

Avraamova, Elena. 2001. "Prospects for Mortgage Lending Developments in Russia," *Russian Economic Trends*, 10:1, pp. 15–19.

Bain, J.A., J.B. Miller, J.R. Thornton and M. Keren. 1978. "The Ratchet, Tautness and Managerial Behaviour in Soviet-Type Economies," *European Economic Review*, 31, pp. 1173–1202.

Barberis, N., M. Boycko, A. Shliefer and N. Twukanova. 1996. "How Does Privatization Work? Evidence from the Russian Shops," *Journal of Political Economy*, 104:4, pp. 764–790.

Bardhan, Pranab. 2004. *International Trade, Growth and Development*, Blackwell.

Barkhatova, N. 2000. "Russian Small Business, Authorities and the State," *Europe–Asia Studies*, 52, pp. 657–676.

Basu, S., S. Estrin and J. Svejnar. 1994. "Employment and Wage Behavior of Enterprises under Communism and in Transition: Evidence from Central Europe And Russia," McGill University. Mimeo.

BBC Monitoring. January 2006. "Original Text of Putin's Annual News Conference for International Journalists," Moscow, p. 2.

Berg, A., E. Borensztein, R. Sahay and J. Zettelmeyer. 1999. "The Evolution of Output in Transition Economies: Explaining the Differences." Working Paper No. WP/99/73, International Monetary Fund, Washington, DC.

Berglof, E. and P. Bolton. 2002. "The Great Divide and Beyond: Financial Architecture in Transition," *Journal of Economic Perspectives*, 16:1, pp. 77–100.

Berglof, Erik, Andrei Kunov, Julia Shvets and Ksenia Yudaeva. 2004. *The New Political Economy of Russia*, The MIT Press.

Berkowitz, Daniel and David Dejong. 2001. "The Evolution of Market Integration in Russia," *Economics of Transition*, 9:1, pp. 87–104.

Berkowitz, D., K. Pistor and J.-F. Richard. 2003. "Economic Development, Legality and Transplant Effect," *European Economic Review*, 47:1, pp. 165–195.

Black, B., R. Krakkman and A. Tarassova. 2000. "Russian Privatization and Corporate Governance: What Went Wrong?" *Stanford Law Review*, 32, pp. 1731–1808.

Blanchard, O. 1997. *The Economics of Post-Communist Reform*, Oxford University Press.

—— 1997. *The Economics of Post-Communist Transition*, Oxford University Press.

Blejer, Mario I. and Marko Skreb. 2002. *Transition: The First Decade*, The MIT Press.

Bolton, P. and G. Roland. 1997. "The Breakup of Nations: A Political Economy Analysis," *Quarterly Journal of Economics*, 112:4, pp. 1056–1090.

Boycko, M., A. Shleifer and R. Vishny. 1995. *Privatizing Russia*, The MIT Press.

Brainerd, E. 1998. "Winners and Losers in Russia's Economic Transition," *American Economic Review*, 88:5, pp. 1094–1115.

Brainerd, Elizabeth and David M. Cutler. Winter 2005. "Autopsy on an Empire: Understanding Mortality in Russia and the Former Soviet Union," *Economic Perspectives*, 19:1, pp. 107–130.

Breslauer, George W. 2002. *Gorbachev and Yeltsin as Leaders*, Cambridge University Press.

Brown, A., B.W. Ickes and R. Ryterman. 1994. "The Myth of Monopoly: A New View of Industrial Structure in Russia," World Bank Policy Research Working Paper, p. 1331.

Brown, J. David and John Earle. 2003. "The Reallocation of Workers and Jobs in Russian Industry." *Economics of Transition*, 11:2, pp. 223–252.

Brown, S. and J. Earle. 2001. "Privatization, Competition and Reform Strategies: Theory and Evidence from Russian Enterprise Panel Data." Working Paper, Stockholm Institute of Transition Economics, Stockholm.

—— 2001. "Competition and Firm Performance: Lessons from Russia." Working Paper, Stockholm Institute of Transition Economics, Stockholm.

Campos, N. and F. Coricelli. 2000. "Growth in Transition: What We Know, What We Don't and What We Should." Paper prepared for project "Explaining Growth." Global Development Networks, Washington, DC.

Cappelletti, M. 1985. "Who Watches the Watchmen? A Comparative Study of Judicial Responsibility," In Eds. S. Shetreet and J. Deschenes, *Judicial Independence: The Contemporary Debate*, Martinus Nijhoff, pp. 550–589.

Center for Economic and Financial Research (CEFIR) and World Bank. 2002. "Monitoring of Administrative Barriers to Small Business Development in Russia, Round 1." Moscow and Washington, DC, Mimeo.

Central Bank of Russia. 2001. *Bulletin of Banking Statistics*, Novosti, Moscow.

Central Election Commission. 2002. "Russian Presidential Elections." www.fci.ru/way/203889/obj/202300.html//.

Cohen, M. 1989. "The Role of Criminal Sanctions in Antitrust Enforcement," *Contemporary Policy Issues*, 7:4, pp. 36–46.

—— 1991. "Explaining Judicial Behavior or What's 'Unconstitutional' about the Sentencing Commission?" *Journal of Law, Economics, and Organization*, 7:1, pp. 183–199.

Claeys, S., G. Lanine and K. Schoors. 2005. "Bank Supervision Russian Style: Rules versus Enforcement and Tacit Objective." William Davidson Institute Working Papers Series wp 778, University of Michigan.

Currie, D. 1998. "Separating Judicial Power," *Law and Contemporary Problems*, 61:3, pp. 7–14.

Dabrowski, Marke, ed. 2004. *Currency Crises in Emerging Markets*, Kluwer.

Das-Gupta, Arindam and Dilip Mookaerjee. 1998. *Incentives and Institutional Reforms in Tax Enforcement: An Analysis of Developing Country Experience*, Oxford University Press, Delhi.

De Melo, M., C. Denizer and A. Gelb. 1997. "From Plan to Market: Patterns of Transition," In Eds. M. Blejer and M. Skreb, *Macroeconomic Stabilization in Transition Economies*, Cambridge University Press, Cambridge, pp. 17–72.

Desai, Padma. Winter 2005. "Russian Retrospectives on Reforms from Yeltsin to Putin," *Economic Perspectives*, 10:1, pp. 87–106.

Djankov, Simeon and Peter Murrell. 2002. "Enterprise Restructuring in Transition: A Quantitative Survey," *Journal of Economic Literature*, XL, pp. 739–792.

Dutta, M. 2002. "Asian Economic Community: Intra-Community Macro- and-Micro Economic Parameters," *Journal of Asian Economics*, 13:4, pp. 447–491.

Earle, J. and K. Sabirianova. 2002. "How Late to Pay? Understanding Wage Arrears in Russia," *Journal of Labor Economics*, 20:3, pp. 661–707.

EBRD. 2003. *Transcript of the Launch of the Transition Report 2003*.

Edlin, B. 1965. *Les Prix Nobel En 1964*, Stockholm.

Eggertsson, Gauti B. and Michael Woodford. 2003. "The Zero Round on Interest Rates and Optimal Monetary Policy," Brookings Papers on Economic Activity, I, pp. 139–211. Strategy of Russia for the Period Ending 2020: Main Provisions. November 2000. Ministry of Energy, Moscow.

Eichengreen, Barry. 2002. *Financial Crisis*, Oxford University Press.

Ericson, R. 2000. "The Post-Soviet Russian Economic System: An Industrial Feudalism?" in Eds. Thomas Komulainen and Iikka Korhonen, *Russian Crisis and Its Effects*, Kikimora Publications, Helsinki, pp. 133–136.

Feng, Yi. 2003. "Democracy, Governance and Economic Performance," *Financial Times*, various issues.

Fisher, S., R. Sahay and C. Vegh. 1996. "Stabilization and Growth in Transition Economies: The Early Experience," *Journal of Economic Perspectives*, 10:2, pp. 45–66.

Freedom House. 2000. "Censor Dot Gov. The Internet and Press Freedom 2000." Washington, DC.

Friebel, G. and S. Guriev. 2000. "Why Russian Workers Do Not Move: Attachment of Workers through In-Kind Payments." Discussion Paper No. 2368, Centre for Economic Policy Research, London.

Frischer, Stanley. 1992. "Russian and the Soviet Union: Then and Now." MIT Working Paper No. 92-00, pp. 1–48.

Fritsch, M. and H. Hansen, eds. 1997. *Rules of Competition and East–West Integration*, Kluwer, Boston, Dordreccht and London.

Frye, T. 2001. "Keeping Shop," In Ed. P. Murrell, *Assessing the Value of Law in Transition Economies*, University of Michigan Press, Ann Arbor, pp. 229–249.

Frye, T. and E. Zhuravskaya. 2000. "Rackets, Regulation and the Rule of the Law," *Journal of Law, Economics and Organization*, 16:2, pp. 478–502.

Gaddy, Clifford G. 1991. *The Price of the Past: Russia's Struggle With the Legacy of a Militarized Economy*, Brookings Institution.

Gaidar, Yegor. 2003. *The Economics of Russian Transition*, The MIT Press.

Gavrilenkov, Evgeny. 1999. "Permanent Crisis in Russia: Selected Problems of Macroeconomic Performance," *Journal of Economics*, 40:1, pp. 41–57.

Glaeser, Edward L. and Andrei Shleifer. 2003. "The Rise of the Regulatory State," *Journal of Economic Literature*, XLI, pp. 401–425.

Gluschenko, Konstantin. 2003. "Market Integration in Russia During the Transformation Years," *Economics of Transition*, 11:3, pp. 411–434.

Goldman, Marshall. 2003. *The Privatization of Russia: Russian Reform Goes Awry*, New York, Routledge.

Gordon, Roger A. and David Li. 1997. "Government Distributional Concerns and Economic Policy During the Transition From Socialism." CEPR Discussion Paper No. 1662.

Grafe, C. and Charles Wyplosz. 1997. "The Real Exchange Rate in Transition Economies." CEPR Discussion Paper No. 1773.

Granville, B. 1995. *The Success of Russian Economic Reforms*, Royal Institute of International Affairs.

Grossman, Gregory. 1998. "Subverted Sovereignty: Historic Role of the Soviet Underground," In Eds. Stephen S. Cohen and Andrew Schwarz, *Tunnel at the End of the Light*, University of California.

Gugler, Klaus, Dennis Mueller and B. Burein Yurtoglu. 2003. "The Impact of Corporate Governance on Investment Returns in Developed and Developing Countries," *Economic Journal*, 113:491, pp. F511–F539.

Guriev, Sergei and Andrei Rachinsky. Winter 2005. "The Role of Oligarchs in Russian Capitalism," *Economic Perspectives*, 19:1, pp. 131–150.

Gurov, Alexander. 1990. *Professinal 'Naia Prestupnost*, Moscow.

Hellman, J. and M. Schankerman. 2000. "Intervention, Corruption, and Capture: The Nexus between Enterprises and the State," *Economics of Transition*, 8:3, pp. 545–576.

Hellman, J., G. Jones and K. Kaufmann. 2000. "Seize the State, Seize the Day: State Capture, Corruption and Influence in Transition." Policy research Working Paper No. 2444, World Bank, Washington, DC.

Hellmann, J., G. Jones, D. Kaufmann and M. Schankerman. 2000. "Measuring Governance and State Capture: The Role of Bureaucrats and Firms in Shaping the Business Environment." Working Paper No. 51, European Bank for Reconstruction and Development, London.

Helpman, Elhanan. 1999. "The Structure of Foreign Trade," *Economic Perspectives*, 13:2, pp. 121–144.

Hendley, K. 2001. "Beyond the Tip of the Iceberg: Business Disputes in Russia," In Ed. P. Murrell, *Assessing the Value of Law in Transition Economies*, University of Michigan Press, Ann Arbor, pp. 20–55.

Hendley, K., P. Murrel and R. Ryterman. 2001. "Law Works in Russia: The Role of Law in Interenterprise Transaction," In Ed. P. Murrell, *Assessing the Value of Law in Transition Economies*, University of Michigan Press, Ann Arbor, pp. 56–93.

Hertel, Thomas W., Paul V. Preckel, Johnn A.L. Cranfield and Maros Ivanic. 2001. "Poverty Impacts of Multilateral Trade Liberalization," Purdue University.

Hessel, M. and K. Murphy. 2000. "Stealing the State, and Everything Else: A Survey Of Corruption in the Postcommunist World." *Transparency International*, March.

Heybey, B. and P. Murrell. 1999. "The Relationship between Economic Growth and the Speed of Liberalization during Transition," *Journal of Policy Reform*, 3:2, pp. 121–137.

IMF. 2000. "Russian Federation: Staff Report for the 2000 Article IV Consultation and Public Information Notice Following Commutation." Staff Country Report 00/145, Washington, DC.

—— 2000. *Report on the Russian Federation.*

—— *World Economic Outlook*, various issues.

Ishaev, V.I. *et al.* 2001. *Concept of Strategic Development of Russia for the Period Ending in 2010*, Moscow.

Johnson, S., J. McMillan and C. Woodruff. 1999. "Entrepreneurs and the Ordering of Institutional Reform: Poland, Romania, Russia, the Slovak Republic and Ukraine Compared." EBRD Working Paper No. 44.

—— 2000. "Courts and Relational Contract." MIT, Stanford University and University of California at San Diego., Mimeo.

Kadotchnikov, Pavel. 2002. "Establishing a Stabilization Fund in Russia," *Russian Economic Trends*, 11:1, pp. 8–17.

Kharas, Homi, Brian Pinot and Sergei Ulatov. 2001. "An Analysis of Russia's

1998 Meltdown: Fundamentals and Market Signals." Brookings Institute Papers on Economic Activity, pp. 1–68.

Kim, S. and A. Horn. 1999. "Regulation Policies Concerning Natural Monopolies in Developing and Transition Countries." DESA Discussion Paper No. 8, United Nations.

Kivikari, Urpo. 2002. "The Northern Dimension – One Pillar of the Bridge Between Russia and the EU," *Russian Economic Trends*, 11:4, pp. 26–30.

Klein, Lawrence R. and Marshall Pomer. 2001. *The New Russia: Transition Gone Awry*, Stanford University.

Klein, Lawrence R., Vladimir Eskin and Andrei Roudoi. 2003–2005. "Current Quarter Model of the Russian Economy and Global Insight," University of Pennsylvania, November 15, 2003, pp. 1–3.

Klitgard, Robert E. 1998. *Controlling Corruption*, University of California.

Knack, S. and P. Keefer. 1995. "Institutions and Economic Performance: Cross-Country Tests Using Alternative Measures," *Economics and Politics*, 7:3, pp. 207–227.

Knigman, Paul and Maurice Obstfeld. 2003. *International Economics*, Foresman.

Kojima, Kiyoshi. 2004. *The Flying Geese Theory of Economic Development*, Tokyo.

Kolenikov, S. and A. Shorrocks. 2001. "Regional Dimensions of Poverty in Russia." Mimeo.

Kontorovich, V. 2001. "The Russian Health Crisis and the Economy," *Communist and Post-Communist Studies*, 34, pp. 221–240.

Kornia, J. 1998. *From Socialism to Capitalism*, Center for Post-Collectivist Studies, London.

Kose, M. Ayhan, Christopher Otrok and Charles H. Whiteman. 2003. "International Business Cycles: World, Region, and Country-Specific Factors," *American Economic Review*, 93:4, pp. 1216–1239.

Kuzminov, Ya. I., S.V. Stephashin, J. Roaf, G.A. Satarov and M. Levin. 2000. "On Corruption," *Conference/Seminar on Investment Climate in Russia's Economic Strategy*, Moscow.

Latynina, Y. 2002. "Osnovy Gosudarstvennogo Feodalizma" [Foundations of State Fedualism], *Nezavisimaya Gaseta*, July 1, 2002.

Letiche, John M., ed. 1992. *International Economic Policies and Their Theoretical Foundations*, Academic Press, pp. 80–84.

Letiche, John M. and Basil Dmytryshyn. 1985. *Russian Statecraft: The Politika of Yurii Krizanich*, Blackwell.

Limonov, Leonid. 2002. "Land Reform and Emerging Property Market in Russia," Newsletter of Lincoln Institute of Land Policy.

Lipton, David, Jeffrey D. Sachs, Vladimir Mau and Edmund S. Phelps. 1992. "Prospects for Russia's Economic Reforms," *Brookings Papers on Economic Activity*, 1992:2, pp. 213–283.

Litwask, J. 2001. "Central Control of Regional Budgets: Theory With Applications to the Russian Federation." OECD Economics Department Working Paper No. 275.

Liuhto, Kari and Jari Jumpponen. 2001. "International Activities of Russian

Corporations – Where Does Russian Business Expansion Lead," *Russian Economic Trends*, 10:3/4, pp. 19–29.
Loungani, Prakash and Paulo Mauro. 2000. "Capital Flight From Russia." IMF Policy Discussion Paper No. 00/06. Washington, DC, IMF (April).
Lvov, D.C. *et al.* 1999. *The Road to the XXI Century*, Russian Academy of Sciences.
McKinsey Global Institute. 1999. *Russian Economy: Growth is Possible*, McKinsey and Co., New York.
Maddison, Angus. 2001. *The World Economy, A Millennial Perspective, 0–1998 AD*, OECD.
Megginson, William L. and Jeffry M. Netter. 2001. "From State to Market: A Survey of Empirical Studies on Privatization," *Journal of Economic Literature*, 39:2, pp. 321–389.
Myerson, Roger B. 2001. "Review of Incentives and Political Economy by Jean-Jacques Laffont," *Journal of Economic Literature*, 39:4, pp. 1277–1279.
National Science Foundation. 2000. *Research and Development in Industry 2000.*
New York Review, various issues.
New York Times, various issues.
Novikov, Vadim. 2002. "Common European Economic Space: The Choice of Space or the Space of Choice?" *Russian Economic Trends*, 11:4, pp. 9–13.
Obstfeld, Maurice. 2004. "Globalization Macroeconomic Performance and the Exchange Rate of the Emerging Economies," *Monetary Economic Studies* (Special Edition/December 2004).
O'Donnel, G. 1998. "Horizontal Accountability in New Democracies," *Journal of Democracy*, 9:3, pp. 112–126.
OECD, *Economic Outlook*, various issues.
—— *Russian Federation: Economic Surveys*, various issues.
—— 2002. *International Trade by Commodity Statistics*, Paris.
Ovcharova, Lilio and Daria Popova. 2001. "What Kind of Poverty Alleviation Policy Does Russia Need?" *Russian Economic Trends*, 10:1, pp 7–14.
Parris, Brett. 1999. *Trade for Development Making the WTO Work for the Poor*, World Vision International.
Persson, Torsten and Guido Tabellini. 2003. *The Economic Effects of Constitutions.*
Pinto, Brian, Vladimir Drebentsov and Alexander Morozov. 2000. "Dismantling Russia's Nonpayment System: Creating Conditions for Growth." World Bank Technical Paper No. 471, Washington, DC.
Popov, V. 2001. "Reform Strategies and Economic Performance of Russia's Regions," *World Development*, 29:5, pp. 865–886.
Putin, Vladimir. 2000–2004. "Annual State-of-the-Nation Address to Russian Parliament."
—— 2001. *First Person*, Public Affairs.
Radygin, Alexander and Sergey Arikhipov. 2001. "Ownership Structure and Financial Position of Firms in Russia; Empirical Analysis," *Russian Economic Trends*, 10:2, pp. 19–26.
Ramseyer, J.M. and E. Rasmusen. 1997. "Judicial Independence in a Civil Law

Regime: The Evidence from Japan," *Journal of Law, Economics, and Organization*, 13:2, pp. 259–286.

Redkin, Vladimir *et al.* 2003. *Russian Economic Trends*, Moscow.

Roland, Gerard. 2000. *Transition and Economics*, The MIT Press.

—— 2002. "The Political Economy in Transition," *Journal of Economic Perspectives*, 16:1, pp. 29–50.

Romer, David. 2003. "Misconceptions and Political Outcomes," *Economic Journal*, 113:484, pp. 1–20.

Rose-Ackerman, Susan. 1999. *Corruption and Government: Causes, Consequences and Reform*, Cambridge University.

Russian Government, "Central Bank Approved Joint Statement on Economy, European Centre for Economic Policy, 2001," *BBC Monitoring.*

Russian-European Centre for Economic Policy. *Russian Economic Trends,* various issues.

Samson, Ivan. 2002. "The Common European Economic Space Between Russia and the EU: An Institutional Anchor for Accelerating Reform," *Russian Economic Trends*, 11:3, pp. 7–15.

Samuelson, Paul A. Summer 2004. "Where Ricardo and Mell Rebut and Confirm Argument of Mainstream Economists Supporting Globalization," *Economic Perspectives*, 18:3, pp 135–146.

Schmidt, K. 2000. "The Political Economy of Mass Privatization and the Risk of Expropriation," *European Economic Review*, 44:2, pp. 393–421.

Schoors, Koen. 2001. *Fate of Russia's Former State Banks: Chronicle of A Restructuring Postponed and a Crisis Foretold*, Ghent University.

Shleifer, A. and D. Treisman. 2000. *Without a Map: Political Tactics and Economic Reform in Russia*, The MIT Press.

Shleifer, A. and R. Visny. 1993. "Corruption," *Quarterly Journal of Economics*, 108:3, pp. 599–617.

Slay, B. and Capelik. 1998. "Natural Monopoly Regulation and Competition Policy in Russia," *Antitrust Bulletin*, Spring, pp. 229–260.

Soos, Karoly, Ekaterina Ivleva and Irina Levina. 2002. "Russian Manufacturing Industry in the Mirror of it Exports to the European Union," *Russian Economic Trends*, 11:3, pp 31–43.

Sutela, Pekka. 2005. "Will Growth in Russia Continue?" *Bank of Finland Bulletin*, 4, p. 18.

Svejnar, Jan. 2002. "Transition Economies: Performance and Challenges," *Journal of Economic Perspectives*, 16:1, pp. 3–28.

Thompson, William. 2000. "Financial Backwardness in Contemporary Perspective: Prospects for the Development of Financial Intermediation in Russia," *Europe-Asia Studies*, 52:4, p. 614.

Treisman, D. November–December 2002. "Russia Renew?" *Foreign Affairs*, 81:6, pp. 58–72.

Truscott, Peter. 2004. *Putin's Progress: A Biography of Russia's Enigmatic President*, Simon Schuster.

Turunen, Jarkko. 2004. "Leaving State Sector Employment in Russia," *Economics of Transition*, 12:1, pp. 129–152.

Venables, Anthony J. 2003. "Winners and Losers From Regional Integration Agreements," *Economic Journal*, 113:490, pp. 747–761.

Vries, J. de. 2000. "Dutch Economic Growth in Comparative Historical Perspective, 1500–2000," *De Economist*, 148:4, pp. 443–467 and sources cited therein.

—— 2001. "Economic Growth Before and After the Industrial Revolution: A Modest Proposal," In Ed. M. Prak, *Early Modern Capitalism*, Routledge, London, pp. 177–194.

Wall Street Journal, various issues.

Whinnery, John R. 1995. "Lasers for Optical Communication," In *The Froelich/Kent Encyclopedia of Telecommunications*, vol. 10, Marcel Dekker, pp. 209–231.

Winters, L. Alan, Neil McCulloch and Andrew McKay. 2004. "Trade Liberalization and Poverty: The Evidence So Far," *Journal of Economic Literature,* XLII, pp. 72–115.

World Bank. 2000. *Global Development Finance*, Washington, DC.

—— 2001. *Transition – The First Ten Years: Analysis and Lessons for Eastern Europe and the Former Soviet Union*, World Bank, Washington, DC.

—— 2004. *Russian Economic Report*, Washington, DC.

WTO. 2003. *WTO Analytical Index*, Berhan Press.

Yavlinsky, Grigory. 2003. "Reforms That Corrupted Russia," *Financial Times*, September 3, 2003, p. 13.

Yudaeva, Ksenia, Konstantin Kozlov, Nataliz Melentieva and Natalia Ponomareva. "Does Foreign Ownership Matter?" *Economics of Transition*, 11:3, pp. 383–409.

Zakaria, Fareed. 1998. "George Bush and Brent Scowcroft, A World Transformed," *New York Times Book Review*, p. 10.

Index

Figures are indicated by bold page numbers and tables by italics.

Printed in the United States
by Baker & Taylor Publisher Services